BaptistWay Adult Bible Teaching Guide®

Jeremiah and Ezekiel
PROPHETS OF JUDGMENT AND HOPE

DON GARNER
BILL MILLER
ROBERT PRINCE
STEVE WYRICK
ROBBY BARRETT
VIVIAN CONRAD
GARY LONG
BRAD WILLIAMSON

BAPTISTWAYPRESS®

Dallas, Texas

Jeremiah and Ezekiel: Prophets of Judgment and Hope—Adult Bible Teaching Guide

BAPTISTWAY PRESS® Leadership Team
Executive Director, Baptist General Convention of Texas: David Hardage
Director, Education/Discipleship Center: Chris Liebrum
Director, Bible Study/Discipleship Team: Phil Miller
Publisher, BaptistWay Press®: Scott Stevens

Publishing consultant and editor: Ross West
Cover and Interior Design and Production: Desktop Miracles, Inc.
Printing: Data Reproductions Corporation

First edition: March 2014

ISBN–13: 978–1–938355–15–8

How to Make the Best Use of *This* Teaching Guide

Leading a class in studying the Bible is a sacred trust. This *Teaching Guide* has been prepared to help you as you give your best to this important task.

In each lesson, you will find first "Bible Comments" for teachers, to aid you in your study and preparation. The three sections of "Bible Comments" are "Understanding the Context," "Interpreting the Scriptures," and "Focusing on the Meaning." "Understanding the Context" provides a summary overview of the entire background passage that also sets the passage in the context of the Bible book being studied. "Interpreting the Scriptures" provides verse-by-verse comments on the focal passage. "Focusing on the Meaning" offers help with the meaning and application of the focal text.

The second main part of each lesson is "Teaching Plans." You'll find two complete teaching plans in this section. The first is called "Teaching Plan—Varied Learning Activities," and the second is called "Teaching Plan—Lecture and Questions." Choose the plan that best fits your class and your style of teaching. You may also use and adapt ideas from both. Each plan is intended to be practical, helpful, and immediately useful as you prepare to teach.

The major headings in each teaching plan are intended to help you sequence how you teach so as to follow the flow of how people tend to learn. The first major heading, "Connect with Life," provides ideas that will help you begin the class session where your class is and draw your class into the study. The second major heading, "Guide Bible Study," offers suggestions for helping your class engage the Scriptures actively and develop a greater understanding of this portion of the Bible's message. The third major heading, "Encourage Application," is meant to help participants focus on how to respond with their lives to this message.

As you begin the study with your class, be sure to find a way to help your class know the date on which each lesson will be studied. You might use one or more of the following methods:

- In the first session of the study, briefly overview the study by identifying with your class the date on which each lesson will be studied. Lead your class to write the date in the table of contents in their *Study Guides* and on the first page of each lesson.
- Make and post a chart that indicates the date on which each lesson will be studied.
- If all of your class has e-mail, send them an e-mail with the dates the lessons will be studied.
- Provide a bookmark with the lesson dates. You may want to include information about your church and then use the bookmark as an outreach tool, too. A model for a bookmark can be downloaded from www.baptistwaypress.org on the Resources for Adults page.
- Develop a sticker with the lesson dates, and place it on the table of contents or on the back cover.

Here are some steps you can take to help you prepare well to teach each lesson and save time in doing so:

1. Start early in the week before your class meets.

2. If your church's adult Bible study teachers meet for lesson overview and preparation, plan to participate. If your church's adult Bible study teachers don't have this planning time now, look for ways to begin. You, your fellow teachers, and your church will benefit from this mutual encouragement and preparation.

3. Overview the study in the *Study Guide*. Look at the table of contents, and see where this lesson fits in the overall study. Then read or review the study introduction to the book that is being studied.

4. Consider carefully the suggested Main Idea, Question to Explore, and Teaching Aim. These can help you discover the main thrust of this particular lesson.

5. Use your Bible to read and consider prayerfully the Scripture passages for the lesson. Using your Bible in your study and in the class

session can provide a positive model to class members to use their own Bibles and give more attention to Bible study themselves. (Each writer of the Bible comments in both the *Teaching Guide* and the *Study Guide* has chosen a favorite translation. You're free to use the Bible translation you prefer and compare it with the translations chosen, of course.)

6. After reading all the Scripture passages in your Bible, then read the Bible comments in the *Study Guide*. The Bible comments are intended to be an aid to your study of the Bible. Read also the small articles—"sidebars"—in each lesson. They are intended to provide additional, enrichment information and inspiration and to encourage thought and application. Try to answer for yourself the questions included in each lesson. They're intended to encourage further thought and application, and you can also use them in the class session itself. Continue your Bible study with the aid of the Bible comments included in this *Teaching Guide*.

7. Review the "Teaching Plans" in this *Teaching Guide*. Consider how these suggestions would help you teach this Bible passage in your class to accomplish the teaching aim.

8. Consider prayerfully the needs of your class, and think about how to teach so you can help your class learn best.

9. Develop and follow a lesson plan based on the suggestions in this *Teaching Guide*, with alterations as needed for your class.

10. Enjoy leading your class in discovering the meaning of the Scripture passages and in applying these passages to their lives.

Adult Online Bible Commentary. Plan to get the additional adult Bible study comments available online. Call 1–866–249–1799 or e-mail baptistway@texasbaptists.org to order *Adult Online Bible Commentary*. It is available only in electronic format (PDF) from our website. The price of these comments is $6 for individuals and $25 for a group of five. A church or class that participates in our advance order program for free shipping can receive *Adult Online Bible Commentary* free. Call 1–866–249–1799 or see www.baptistwaypress.org for information on participating in our free shipping program for the next study.

Adult Online Teaching Plans. An additional teaching plan is also available in electronic format (PDF) by calling 1–866–249–1799. The price of these plans for an entire study is $5 for an individual or $20 for a group of five. It is available only in electronic format (PDF) from our website. A church or class that participates in our advance order program for free shipping can receive *Adult Online Teaching Plans* free. Call 1–866–249–1799 or see www.baptistwaypress.org for information on participating in our free shipping program for the next study.

FREE! Downloadable teaching resource items for use in your class are available at www.baptistwaypress.org! Watch for them in "Teaching Plans" for each lesson. Then go online to www.baptistwaypress.org and click on "Teaching Resource Items" for this study. These items are selected from "Teaching Plans." They are provided online to make lesson preparation easier for hand-outs and similar items. Permission is granted to download these teaching resource items, print them out, copy them as needed, and use them in your class.

IN ADDITION: Enrichment teaching help is provided in the online *Baptist Standard,* which is available at www.baptiststandard.com. The *Baptist Standard* is available online for an annual subscription rate of $10. Subscribe online at www.baptiststandard.com or call 214–630–4571. A free ninety-day trial subscription is currently available.

Note: The time of the first release of these materials includes Easter. To meet the needs of churches who wish to have a Bible study lesson specifically on the Easter Scripture passages at this time, an Easter lesson is included.

Writers of This Teaching Guide

William C. Miller, writer of "Bible Comments" for lessons one through four, is pastor of First Baptist Church of Farmington, Missouri. Dr. Miller is a graduate of Midwestern Baptist Theological Seminary in Kansas City. He has been active in Baptist life in Missouri and has written several assignments for BAPTISTWAY PRESS®. He also teaches the college-age Sunday School department at First Baptist Church. He and his wife Mary Beth's two sons, daughters-in-law, and granddaughters live in Fayetteville, Arkansas.

Brad Williamson wrote "Teaching Plans" for lessons one through three. Dr. Williamson is minister of education at South Main Baptist Church, Pasadena, Texas. He has taught adults in Sunday School for more than twenty years and is a frequent contributing writer for BAPTISTWAY PRESS®. In addition to his church responsibilities, he has served as an adjunct professor for Southwestern Seminary, Logsdon Seminary, and the B.H. Carroll Theological Institute.

Stephen Von Wyrick wrote "Bible Comments" for lessons five through eight. Dr. Wyrick serves as professor of Hebrew Bible and Archaeology at the University of Mary-Hardin Baylor, Belton, Texas, and as lecturer in religion at Baylor University. He has written numerous assignments for BAPTISTWAY PRESS®.

Robby Barrett wrote "Teaching Plans" for lessons four through six. Robby is minister of education at First Baptist Church, Amarillo, Texas. He has written numerous teaching plans for BAPTISTWAY PRESS®.

Gary Long wrote lessons seven and eight and the Easter lesson in the *Adult Bible Study Guide* and also "Teaching Plans" for these lessons in this *Adult Bible Teaching Guide*. Gary and his family live in Cullowhee, North Carolina. He works for Baptist Standard Publishing of Dallas, Texas, with their online faith-based community called *FaithVillage*

(faithvillage.com) and also promotes the *Baptist Standard's* new print monthly named *CommonCall* (see baptiststandard.com). Gary formerly served as pastor of First Baptist Church, Gaithersburg, Maryland, and before that Willow Meadows Baptist Church, Houston, Texas. He has also served churches in North Carolina and Virginia.

Robert Prince, writer of "Bible Comments" for lessons nine and ten and the Easter lesson, serves as senior pastor of First Baptist Church, Waynesville, North Carolina. A native of Georgia, Dr. Prince has also served pastorates in that state and in Texas. He has also served as an adjunct instructor at Southwestern and New Orleans Baptist Theological Seminaries, and at Wayland Baptist University. He earned his B.A. degree from Baylor University, and his M.Div. and Ph.D. degrees from Southwestern Baptist Theological Seminary. He has written several other assignments for BAPTISTWAY PRESS®.

Don Garner wrote "Bible Comments" on lessons eleven through thirteen. Dr. Garner teaches Old Testament and biblical archaeology at Carson-Newman College, Jefferson City, Tennessee. He has served various Baptist churches as pastor, interim pastor, Bible teacher, and retreat leader. He has written a number of other assignments for BAPTISTWAY PRESS®.

Vivian Conrad wrote lessons nine through thirteen in the *Adult Bible Study Guide* and the accompanying teaching plans in this *Adult Bible Teaching Guide*. After teaching Old Testament and biblical studies for twelve years at an international Christian school in the Philippines, she now serves as executive director of Mineral Wells Senior Center, Mineral Wells, Texas. She holds degrees in Christian Education and Theology from Dallas Baptist University and Southwestern Baptist Theological Seminary. Vivian and her husband are active in the music and teaching ministry of Clear Fork Baptist Church in Azle, Texas.

Jeremiah and Ezekiel: Prophets of Judgment and Hope

Visions of God's Truth

FOCAL TEXT
Jeremiah 1

BACKGROUND
Jeremiah 1

MAIN IDEA
God called and commissioned
Jeremiah to do a difficult
task, promising to deliver him
in spite of all opposition.

QUESTION TO EXPLORE
To what task—difficult or
easy—is God calling you?

TEACHING AIM
To lead adults to summarize
God's call to Jeremiah
and to testify of their
experiences with God's call

LESSON ONE
Commissioned to Deliver God's Message

BIBLE COMMENTS

Understanding the Context

Jeremiah likely was born during the end of the reign of Manasseh, one of the worst kings in Judah's history (reigned 647–642 B.C.). Jeremiah's ministry began during the reign of King Josiah, in 626 B.C. (see Jeremiah 1:2). He witnessed the demise of Judah at the hands of the Babylonians in 587 B.C.

Jeremiah was a man of great courage. He preached against the evil of the day and against corrupt religion. His was the unenviable position of declaring that the national threat coming from Babylon was God's judgment. Consider how one might view such a person today.

As with all the prophets, the concept of "the word of the LORD" was crucial (Jer. 1:2). The "word" was their message and their burden. So compelling was the "word" that it was impossible to keep silent. But, that "word" resulted in considerable hardship for Jeremiah.

Still, silence was not an option because the "word" came from the Lord. I recall one of my professors commenting on the *call to preach* and saying that if there were anything else we could do, we should do it. The implication was that the nature of this vocation truly requires a call from God.

We see this in Jeremiah's call. No doubt, he did not welcome the conflict, abuse, torment, and hatred of his fellow citizens. But he had no choice. Did he feel that the destiny of a nation rested with him and his message from God? Unless the people heard, believed, and obeyed God's "word" that Jeremiah spoke, the nation would be lost.

In many ways, we have a similar calling. A great responsibility rests on us. In Jeremiah, we see the example we can follow.[1]

Interpreting the Scriptures

Difficult Days (1:1–3)

Hilkiah was a priest in Anathoth. Jeremiah was of a priestly lineage; however, we do not know whether he ever served as a priest. He was highly critical of the priests.

Jeremiah's prophetic ministry spanned four decades. These verses introduce the book and Jeremiah's ministry. A recurring theme is "the word of the LORD" (1:2). The "word" Jeremiah spoke came from God.

Jeremiah's message was often harsh. It was always direct. But clarity was necessary in view of the imminent danger the people faced in their spiritual rebellion.

God has typically done his work and spread his message through people. Jeremiah was God's called servant to deliver the message. He did so against fierce opposition in obedience to God's divine call.

A Reluctant Prophet (1:4–10)

1:4. "Now the word of the Lord came to me." It is a serious error for pastors, Bible study leaders, or anyone else to mistake their own words for "the word of the LORD." Likely, we do not experience the same type of revelation that came to Jeremiah. However, we do have the Bible. With the Bible, and with the guidance of God's Spirit, we then can interpret and help people apply God's word to their lives. However, interpretation and proclamation require great humility.

1:4–5. Four strong verbs appear in these verses. Each carries a compelling, contemporary message.

God "knew" Jeremiah before he was conceived. God "formed" him in the womb. God knows us, and the assumption in this verse is that God loved us before we were born.

God "consecrated" Jeremiah. Consecration has to do with a unique purpose and with holiness. Holiness in a person or an object comes from one's relationship to God. God sets an individual apart for his service.

God "appointed" Jeremiah as "a prophet to the nations." While Jeremiah did not physically travel throughout the world, his words reverberated in nations far away from Jerusalem. Those words continue to speak today.

1:6. With God's strong actions in verse 5, there was a corresponding response from Jeremiah. In some ways, Jeremiah's reaction was appropriate as he considered reasons God should not call him. His reaction was not an excuse. It was a legitimate concern at his perceived inadequacy for such a huge task. This was reminiscent of Moses' response to God's call.[2] Jeremiah's reaction may be similar to some of our feelings as well.

Why would God call an individual for such a task? In the same way, to say that one is called to a Christian vocation would seem unreasonable were it not for the deep-seated conviction that such a vocation requires the call of God. A crucial question for every church I have served as pastor has been, *Has God called you to this work?*

1:7–8. God offered assurance to his reluctant prophet by pointing out that the call was to God's mission. Here is another reminder for the ages. Jeremiah's mission was not his own. It belonged to God. God gave the direction, and God would give the words. Proverbs 3:5–6 expresses this well.

God's second assurance to Jeremiah was, "Do not be afraid of them." The people of God find help, hope, and courage in these words. Three times in Joshua 1:1–10, God said to Joshua, "Be strong and courageous" (Joshua 1:6, 7, 9). Jeremiah's task was as daunting as Joshua's. Knowing the promise of God to those men encourages us as well.

The source of Jeremiah's courage was the presence of the Lord. For the believer, the corollary to "Do not be afraid," will always be, *For I (the Lord) am with you.*

God did not send the prophet on mission alone. God would go with him. To Christians, Jesus said, "I am with you always, even to the end of the age" (Matthew 28:20).

1:9–10. In a sense these verses summarize the first eight verses. In a symbolic gesture the prophet said that God touched his mouth. God put his words in the mouth of the prophet whom he had appointed.

Then the Lord described the power of that divine word. It could destroy and tear down. Such awesome power would reveal itself in the Babylonian conquest of Judah.

That word would also have power to build and to plant. To hear, to believe, and to obey God's word in repentance and in faith would result in new life for the people and for the nation.

Although Jeremiah might have been a reluctant prophet, Jeremiah's obedience to the call of God did impact the nations.

A Hard Message (1:11–17)

1:11–12. The people of that day sometimes referred to the almond tree as the *wake or awakening tree.* It was the first to bloom in spring. Like the dogwood in Missouri, it signaled the advent of spring. For us, that is good news.

For Jeremiah and for the people, the news was not good. The people had disobeyed too long. Perhaps they somehow believed God had forgotten or would overlook their sin. But, God saw Judah's sin. He did not forget. He still knows.

God watches over his "word to perform it." It will have its desired effect, positive and negative. God also watches over his faithful servant as that servant engages in the conflict.

1:13. It would not have been unusual in that day to see a pot of some kind over an open fire, boiling water. My maternal grandparents lived deep in the Missouri Ozarks. Grandma frequently used a kettle over an open fire to boil water. That boiling water served a variety of purposes.

In Jeremiah's account, the pot was tilted precariously to the south, toward Judah. It is not difficult to see the disaster this represented.

1:14. Who was the enemy who would come from the north? Jeremiah did not here identify it. Since Assyrian power had waned, the people might have paid little attention to his prophecy.

Even though geographically Babylon was east of Judah, because of terrain their route of conquest might have taken a circuitous route so they invaded from the north. Ultimately, Babylon was the enemy Judah should have feared.

1:15–17. Whomever the physical enemy Jeremiah envisioned, God made it clear to Jeremiah, who in turn told the people, that God himself was initiating this judgment.

The destruction Babylon would bring was a judgment on a sinful people. In verse 16 Jeremiah made clear both God's act and God's reasons for the judgment.

This message was a difficult message to deliver. No one would want this responsibility.

The Promise of God (1:18–19)

In verse 17 God exhorted Jeremiah to have courage. In verse 18 God promised Jeremiah that he would give him strength. Jeremiah would need it because he would have to go "against the whole land." It would have been an overwhelming assignment. As verse 18 indicates, the people would not welcome Jeremiah's message. They would actively oppose it.

Christians sometimes feel we face similar obstacles. However, we too can know the confidence and the assurance that God gave to Jeremiah. Whatever God gives us to do, we can know, "'. . . they will not overcome you, for I am with you to deliver you,' declares the LORD."

Focusing on the Meaning

Jeremiah is a crucial book for both Old and New Testament study. It is also a difficult book to read and to study. As I wrote this, several in our church were nearing the end of praying through Jeremiah. Meditating on this book gives one the opportunity to consider deeply the spiritual situations Jeremiah foreshadowed in the first chapter.

Unfaithfulness then, and now, on the part of God's people is a cause for alarm. God had been patient. The people had seen an example of God's judgment on Israel. Still they strayed from God.

The message God gave to Jeremiah was direct and severe. Judgment was coming, and God's prophet had to deliver that message. The only hope for the people was to repent.

Is a people ever too far gone for redemption? God is patient and loving. He continued to send prophets to the people. He still sends messengers with the good news. He is a compassionate God who wants people to be saved.

Then and now, God called people to serve him. That service was not easy, but the servant can expect God's grace, strength, and help. Jeremiah faced obstacles that caused him great suffering. Still, he was faithful, and so must we be. Jeremiah trusted the Lord. So should we.

One further question arises in this study of Jeremiah. Is serving God worth the cost? God is present with his people. Ultimately, God will not allow evil to overcome his servants. Jeremiah must have wondered why he must continue to take God's message to such rebellious people. He sometimes wanted to run away. But, he was faithful. For Jeremiah, and for us, the call and the leading of God are important. Success in the kingdom of God is in one's faithfulness. Jeremiah is an example for us of such faithfulness.

TEACHING PLANS

Teaching Plan—Varied Learning Activities

Preparation: Before the class session, enlist someone from your class to help you with an impromptu drama. The person will interrupt the lesson with a pretend phone call. Instruct the person to secretly dial your cell phone shortly after the lesson begins. Practice the phone call to make sure it works.

Connect with Life

1. Begin by giving a brief, general introduction to the Book of Jeremiah using information in the *Study Guide*. While you are talking, the class member you have enlisted will secretly dial your cell phone so that it rings out loud in class. Act surprised. Check your phone, and say to your class, *Oh, this call is really important. I've GOT to take it.* Pretend to listen to the other person on the phone and make brief statements like, *Yes, really? I've got it. Hey, can you call me back after Bible study? Thanks. Bye.* Hang up and then proceed to say: *I'm so sorry for that interruption.* (Pause.) Say: *Imagine that*

was God calling and God had something for me to do. I couldn't miss that phone call!

2. Say: *When God has something for us to do, God probably isn't going to call on the phone. It might be nice if God did!* Ask: *Think back to the time when you gave your life to Jesus. How did God get your attention and let you know he was calling you?* (Instruct the class to share answers with the person next to them.) (Possible responses: a sermon; a Bible passage; kept you awake at night; God used a friend or a complete stranger.)

3. Say: *This lesson's Bible study is about responding to God's call. Our example is a young man in the Bible named Jeremiah.* Ask: *What did you think when I took that phone call earlier?* (Encourage feedback.)

Guide Bible Study

4. Call for someone to read aloud Jeremiah 1:1–3. Using comments from the *Study Guide*, finish introducing the Book of Jeremiah (previously started in step 1).

5. State: *As we look at Jeremiah's unique experience, imagine being Jeremiah. Try to put yourself in his shoes.* Enlist someone to read verses 4–5. Ask: *Do you think Jeremiah felt more honored or more afraid?* (Discuss.) Have a volunteer read verse 6. Ask: *What was Jeremiah's response?* (Fear because of his young age. What will people say or think? They won't listen.)

6. Say: *Let's see how God worked in order to equip and help Jeremiah.* Assign the following verses to individuals or pairs so that everyone has an assignment: Verses 7–8; Verses 9–10; Verses 11–12; Verses 13–15; Verse 16; Verse 17–19. Assignment: Discover and describe from your assigned verse or verses how God worked to equip and help Jeremiah. (Allow time for discovery.) Call for reports. (Answers will vary. Affirm each individual while discussing their answers). List answers on the board as they are named, such as these: God gave specific instructions; God promised protection; God strengthened with his touch; God told Jeremiah what to say; God commissioned Jeremiah; God gave visual illustrations of what

he was going to do; God revealed himself to Jeremiah; God encouraged Jeremiah for the task; God reminded Jeremiah that he was only the messenger; God expected obedience from Jeremiah.

Encourage Application

7. Take a hand survey with these questions: *How many have a landline home phone? How many have only a cell phone?* Ask: *What calls do you take, and what calls do you let go to voice mail? Why?*

8. Ask: *What if God wanted our class to start a new ministry? How do you think God would let us know? Would God call on a phone?* (Discuss.) *How do you think we would go about starting this new ministry?* (Option: Share the ministry idea in the small article, "God's Call to You," in the *Study Guide*.) Lead the group to discuss these questions: *Is there a need in our community or church you have heard about? Ministries are about meeting needs. How could God use us to meet this need? Every ministry must have a leader, someone who has the vision and will see it through to the end.*

Teaching Plan—Lecture and Questions

Connect with Life

1. Give these instructions: *With your neighbor, briefly share how you came to choose the profession or job you are or were in.* (Allow two or three people to respond to this question to the whole group.)

2. Ask: *What if God came and told you he had a different job for you to do? How do you think you would react or respond?* (Encourage response.)

3. Say: *This lesson's Bible study is about hearing and responding to God's call. We look at the example of a young man named Jeremiah.*

Guide Bible Study

4. Post the headings from the *Study Guide* on a markerboard. Refer to heading one, "Assigned to God's People (1:1–3)." Enlist someone to read Jeremiah 1:1–3. Using *Study Guide* information, briefly introduce the setting for Jeremiah's prophecy. State that while these are Jeremiah's words, they are more importantly "the word of the LORD" given to Jeremiah.

5. Refer to the second heading, "Appointed for God's Purpose" (1:4–10). Have a volunteer read verses 4–5. State: *God called Jeremiah and let him know he had a special task for Jeremiah to do. This task was the very reason God created Jeremiah. What we imagined earlier (steps 1–2) is exactly what happened to Jeremiah. God has also chosen to use us in this world.* The *Study Guide* says, "Before you were ever born, God had a perfect purpose and plan for your life." Ask: *How would you explain this concept or calling to a teenager or a new believer in Christ?* (Encourage responses. Answers may be slow in coming since this is a hard question. Wait or rephrase the question in order to gain response.)

6. Point out that verse 6 shows Jeremiah's initial response. Read verse 6. State: *We don't know Jeremiah's exact age, but we do know that Jeremiah initially hesitated in responding to God's call. We can all probably relate to Jeremiah's hesitation. Let's see the Lord's response.* Have a volunteer read verses 7–10. Ask: *What was God's response?* As answers are given, briefly discuss each answer. (Possible answers: *I won't take no for an answer; you must obey me; don't be afraid, for I will be with you; I will protect you; the Lord touched Jeremiah's mouth and gave him words to say; God gave Jeremiah a job to do.*)

7. Refer to heading three, "Affirmed by God's Presence (1:11–19)." State: *When God calls us to do something, God will be with us and equip us for the task or opportunity. Let's see how God did that for Jeremiah.* Have a volunteer read verses 11–12. Briefly explain from the *Study Guide* how the almond tree was proof that God was watching over both the nation of Israel and over Jeremiah. Enlist a volunteer to read verses 13–14 (and optionally verses 15–16). State: *God showed Jeremiah what he (God) was about to do. God made sure Jeremiah understood. Similarly, when God calls us to action,*

God is going to be with us, instruct us, and make sure we understand what he wants us to do.

8. Read verses 17–19 (energetically and forcefully, trying to convey the feelings behind these words). Say: *It's almost like God was the coach and Jeremiah the player. God wanted to motivate and encourage Jeremiah for the task.*

Encourage Application

9. Ask: *How would we explain to a teenager how God leads or calls a person to a career or occupation?* Invite discussion. Ask: *How does God call us to get involved in ministry?* (Teacher should be prepared to share his or her calling to teach.)

NOTES

1. Unless otherwise indicated, all Scripture quotations in lessons 1–4 are from the New American Standard Bible (1995 edition).
2. See Exodus 3:11, 13; 4:1, 10, 13.

FOCAL TEXT
Jeremiah 7:1–16

BACKGROUND
Jeremiah 7:1—8:3; 26:1–24

MAIN IDEA
Jeremiah delivered God's
message that the people
were deceiving themselves
by believing they had a
special claim on God even
as they engaged in practices
that disregarded the true
worship and service of God.

QUESTION TO EXPLORE
In what deceptive words
about God are we trusting?

TEACHING AIM
To lead the class to identify
the false religious practices
for which God condemned
Judah and to evaluate how
they apply to our day

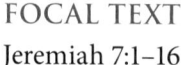

LESSON TWO
*Hear God's
Message*

BIBLE COMMENTS

Understanding the Context

At the risk of his life, Jeremiah preached what is called his *temple sermon.* Chapter 26 likely refers to this sermon also. However, it is possible that Jeremiah gave this or a similar sermon many times.

Jeremiah described the deficiencies in the people's practice of their religion. He noted the commands they had broken. He gave them guidance for repenting and correctly expressing their faith—guidance they ignored.

The people of Judah presumed on their special relationship with God. They ignored the commandments. Their worship was corrupt and unacceptable. They substituted the rituals of religion for obedience to God.

King Josiah, on discovering the book of the law (2 Kings 22; 2 Chronicles 34), had instituted reforms. But Josiah died in battle with the Egyptians (2 Kgs. 23:29–30). The spiritual reforms died with him.

Assyria was no longer a threat. Now Babylon, an even greater concern, loomed on the horizon. Judah's inept political and religious leadership could not lead the people to avoid the coming disaster. The Egyptians removed Josiah's son, Jehoahaz, and installed another son, Jehoiakim, as king.

In trying, uneasy, frightening times, to what do people turn for security and hope? In the case of the people of Judah, it was the temple. There, regardless of their attitudes and behavior, they somehow believed they would be safe.

Jeremiah's message shattered this notion. His was a message of judgment—but also of hope if the people would change. His courage and his faith serve as an example for believers today.

Interpreting the Scriptures

The Authority of the Message and the Messenger (7:1–2)

As the oldest of three brothers, growing up I felt some obligation (and innate right) to tell my younger brothers what to do. Typically, they did not share this attitude. Still, each of us was happy to give instructions to the others. When the other brothers balked or asked, *Who said?* there was a particular satisfaction in being able to say, *Mom or Dad said.*

With those words the messenger and the message had the necessary authority to issue the instruction. The others would then comply.

The word that came to Jeremiah was from the Lord. In verse 2 this message is again described as "the word of the LORD." The message had power and authority and would mean either judgment or hope to the people who heard it.

For a message to be received, the messenger must also be recognized as having authority to deliver that message. If the people would not listen to the messenger, they would give little credence to the message. Jeremiah had the authority. God sent him with his word. But, the people would not listen to Jeremiah. Thus they would not hear, believe, or obey the message.

The Content of God's Message (7:3–7)

7:3. Effective communicators get to the point. As Jeremiah continued the message, he said, "thus says the LORD of hosts, the God of Israel." This is a variation of the "word of the LORD" pronouncements.

The message was both hope and warning. If the people would change their ways, they would continue in the land. Unfortunately, the people had given no historical evidence that they would change their ways—or that they believed they needed to change.

7:4. The people did trust in something. The words in this verse seem like a mantra spoken by the people. They believed they were the people of God. The temple was the house of God. As long as they frequented the temple and kept up the religious ritual, they felt safe.

While our situation is different, it is not difficult to apply this truth. Trusting in religious ritual that people have made empty of meaning does not make one right with God. As a Bible study teacher in the college department, I often broach the subject of religious activity versus true faith and obedience to God.

7:5–7. "For if you truly amend your ways" implies what Jeremiah would later say outright. Their ways and deeds were contrary to God's purpose. They were moving further from God.

For Jeremiah, correct behavior was, first, right actions toward other people. It was not simply religious activity but appropriate ethical behavior in relation to others that demonstrated godliness. Practicing justice is a crucial Old Testament concept. We might define this as *treating people the right way.*

Verse 6 is specific about the expected behavior. The groups Jeremiah named were among the most easily oppressed and yet of the greatest concern to God.[1] The New Testament continues this concern when it says, "Pure and undefiled religion in the sight of our God and Father is this: to visit orphans and widows in their distress, and to keep oneself unstained by the world" (James 1:27).

Verse 7 is a promise of hope. Although it was late, it was not too late if the people would change. That hope foreshadowed Jesus' description of the judgment in Matthew 25:31–46.

No Substitute for God's Message (7:8–11)

7:8. The "deceptive words" were from their spiritual leaders. What happens when those who speak for God do not tell the truth? False prophets and priests were frequent targets for harsh condemnation from God's true prophets.

7:9–10. Jeremiah offered examples of at least six violations of the Ten Commandments. For Jeremiah, it was not that attention to the temple and to sacrifices was unimportant. But, the people had substituted these observances for the more difficult responsibility of obedience. They violated the laws that were intended to protect their neighbors: stealing, murder, adultery, bearing false witness.

They also broke the first two commandments. They placed false gods before God. They offered worship to idols. Thus, they broke the two commands that Jesus offered in summary of all the commands: they loved neither God nor their neighbors.

Still, verse 11 says they came to God's house, performed religious acts, and claimed righteousness only to leave and repeat their sin. This is a powerful, biblical call to shed hypocrisy and be truly devoted to God. As Bible study leaders who each week are in the spotlight, we must first give attention to our own lives. Then, we must make clear how important this message is to us all. Following Jesus is more than attending the requisite number of church services, participating in certain church activities, and occasionally reading the Bible. To follow Jesus is to obey Jesus. That obedience includes ethical behavior and service to others.

7:11. This verse is familiar from Jesus' lament when he cleansed the temple (Matthew 21:12–13). One cannot choose a life of rejecting the word of God and then run to the sacred place to go through the motions as if God does not notice. "Behold, I, even I, have seen it," should have been warning enough to get the people's attention. Jeremiah's words did get their attention, but their reaction was all wrong.

Ignoring God's Message (7:12–16)

7:12. Shiloh was approximately twenty miles north of Jerusalem. It had been the center of worship and was associated with Eli, Samuel, and the ark, but the Philistines had destroyed the city. If, because of the people's unfaithfulness, God would allow Shiloh to be destroyed, they should have realized that Jerusalem could experience the same fate.

7:13–15. Although the focal passage deals with Jeremiah 7:1–16, the entire chapter and chapter 26 are important. The best outcome of Jeremiah's message would have been that the people would repent and turn to God.

They did not. God had been patient and persistent. God said, "I spoke to you, rising up early and speaking." They did not listen (Jer. 7:27). In Jeremiah 26:10–11 they were incensed that Jeremiah would compare Jerusalem to Shiloh. The priests and the prophets who had given strong leadership in the wrong direction would not lead the people to repent. Instead, they wanted to kill Jeremiah, the true messenger from God.

7:16. The focal passage concludes with one of the saddest verses in the Bible. It seems the people's fate was sealed—not because God was not compassionate, but because they would not listen to him.

We cannot use this verse to assume that God instructs us not to pray for people. We are to keep praying. Judgment will always be in God's hands. But, the passage does serve as a warning to those who refuse to "Hear God's Message," and to obey.

Focusing on the Meaning

When I received this writing assignment I was approaching the end of praying through the book of Jeremiah. We list Scriptures in our weekly bulletin for people who wish to join us in praying through the Scriptures. We alternated Jeremiah every two weeks with John. The two books served as a welcome counterbalance.

Jeremiah is a difficult book. It is difficult because the message is harsh. It is also difficult because, reading it all these years later, we know the outcome could have been entirely different had the people listened to God's word and obeyed.

It is hard also because we can see so many contemporary applications. For the people, the presence of the temple and its rituals covered their arrogance, their hypocrisy, and their sins. On the other hand, they did not seem to acknowledge any sin in the first place. How does one repent and find an appropriate relationship with God if he or she is unwilling to acknowledge any need for God? The people of Judah apparently knew how to be religious. But, they did not practice faithfulness.

Further, Jeremiah is hard because it requires our own self-examination. The title of this lesson is "Hear God's Message." People in your Bible study class will have varying degrees of familiarity with the Bible. Because the Bible is God's word, to read it is to hear God. However, truly hearing God's word requires an appropriate response. Repentance, faith, trust, hope, obedience—all are appropriate responses to that hearing. In our Bible study classes, can we find a way to help people receive this message and determine how they are hearing and obeying God's message?

Change in our lives may be necessary. Difficult though it may be, Jeremiah's message is also one of hope. A God of love who is patient and unwilling for any to perish continues to offer hope to those who will walk with him.

TEACHING PLANS

Teaching Plan—Varied Learning Activities

Connect with Life

1. Say, *Do you know what the word "oxymoron" means? An oxymoron is two words or thoughts said together, but they don't really go together; the words are contradictions. Search for "oxymoron" on your smart phone or think of some of your own.* (Example: deafening silence; pretty ugly.) Ask: *Is "rebellious Christian" an oxymoron? Why or why not?* (Encourage debate.)

2. State: *This lesson's Bible study looks at some of the actions of God's people in the Old Testament. The Israelites were enjoying the privileges of being God's people, but their actions toward others didn't match God's expectations. They were another oxymoron: "Covenant breakers."*

Guide Bible Study

3. State: *In lesson 1 on Jeremiah 1, we saw that God called Jeremiah to deliver God's message. In this lesson on Jeremiah 7, God called Jeremiah to go to the entrance to the temple and "welcome" people to worship. Let's read Jeremiah's "welcome" to the worshippers.* Have a volunteer read Jeremiah 7:1–3. Ask: *If we were greeted in this manner on our way to worship, what do you think would be the response?* (Encourage discussion.) Say: *Let's discover why God told Jeremiah to say these things.*

4. Form three discussion groups with the following assignments.[2] (A copy of the assignments is available in "Teaching Resource Items" for this study at www.baptistwaypress.org.)

Group 1: Read silently Jeremiah 7:4–10. (1) Make a list of the offenses God had against the people of Judah. (2) Compare these offenses to the Ten Commandments (see Exodus 20). (3) Which commandments did the Israelites appear to break? (4) How would you summarize the offenses of the Israelites? Be ready to share your findings with the large group.

Group 2: (1) When you think of *home*, what are your expectations? Discuss as a group. (2) Afterwards, read silently Jeremiah 7:1–16, looking for the many words and ways Jeremiah described God's house. (3) Discuss as a group: When you think of God's house, what do you think are God's expectations? Be ready to share your findings with the large group.

Group 3: Silently read Jeremiah 7:12–16. (1) Read the small article, "Shiloh," in the *Study Guide*. Note that God allowed the tabernacle in Shiloh to be destroyed because God's people did not obey him. Jeremiah declared that the temple in Jerusalem would be destroyed for the same reason. (2) In what ways do Christ-followers today take advantage of faith as "grace" and "forgiveness," without affirming that faith is also about "holiness" and "Christlikeness" in their conduct? (Discuss as a group.) Be ready to share your findings with the large group.

5. Allow groups time to work. Call everyone back to the large group and allow each group to present their findings. Using information from the *Study Guide* and "Bible Comments" in this *Teaching Guide*, supplement group reports as needed. Note that the Israelites thought that as long as they came to worship at the temple, they felt they had no other obligations towards God. They wanted the privilege of being God's people but not the responsibility.

Encourage Application

6. Continue the discussion begun in the report of Group 3. Have someone read aloud Ephesians 2:8–10 and someone else read James

2:14–19. Ask, *What do these two New Testament Scripture readings add to our discussion?*

7. Lead the class to consider silently how they are balancing being the recipients of God's grace with the responsibilities that come as being followers of Christ. Conclude with prayer.

Teaching Plan—Lecture and Questions

Connect with Life

1. Ask your class to think back, visualizing and retracing their steps today, and identify how many times they were greeted on the way to Bible study, from the parking lot to the building, to the classroom. (Allow time for thought.) Afterwards, have everyone share their name and how many times they were greeted. Ask: *What was the most common form of greeting you experienced today?* (Examples: handshake; someone opened the door; hug; conversation.)

2. Say: *Suppose instead that our minister was standing at the entrance and rather than welcoming you, said:* [read boldly] *"The Lord says: Reform your ways and your actions; then you may enter this place."* Ask: *What do you think would have been your response?* (Encourage discussion.)

Guide Bible Study

3. Say: *That greeting we just discussed came from Jeremiah 7:3. It was part of Jeremiah's "temple sermon." Jeremiah's words are not the way we think about being greeted at church. Yet that is precisely what God told Jeremiah to say to the Israelites as they approached his temple.* (Have someone read Jeremiah 7:1–3.) Ask: *What do you suppose was going on in Israel that God would have prompted Jeremiah to share such a message?* (Allow for guesses or responses.)

4. Direct the class to search Jeremiah 7:6–11 silently to discover the reasons for Jeremiah's words. Ask, *What were the people of Judah doing that so offended God?* (Allow time for reading.)

5. Call for responses, making a list of the offenses of the Israelites. (List answers on the board under the headings "Against God" and "Against others.") Ask: *Which of these offenses would you classify as the worst?* (Encourage discussion.) Point out that the Israelites were breaking at least six of the Ten Commandments (commandments 8, 6, 7, 9, 2, and 1; see Exod. 20:1–17; Deut. 5:6–21).

6. Say: *Perhaps the worst offense might have been that the people knowingly participated in sinful actions and yet thought it was fine to approach God's temple expecting God's blessing.* (Read Jer. 7:4, 10–11.) Use information in the *Study Guide* and "Bible Comments" in this *Teaching Guide* to describe briefly the offenses and God's response. Point out that the people of Judah thought the temple represented good standing with God. They wanted the privileges of being connected to God, but they didn't want the responsibilities that went with the covenant relationship.

7. Point out that in order to correct their thinking and actions, Jeremiah recalled another familiar time in Israel's history. Enlist someone to read Jeremiah 7:12–16. Use information in the *Study Guide* to clarify what happened in Shiloh, as well as why God wasn't willing to respond to the people's insincere prayers.

Encourage Application

8. Say: *Jeremiah's "temple sermon" focused on the sinfulness of the worshipers. Sin isn't something we like to discuss, especially when it's our own. Let's think about sin in general terms.* Ask: *Concerning our relationships towards others, what do even Christians sometimes do that potentially harms others and offends God?* (Encourage responses.) Ask: *In what ways do you think Christians' actions throughout the week affect church attendance and worship on Sundays?* (Encourage responses.)

9. Remind the class that Jeremiah 7:11 says, in effect, that God is watching. We cannot hide anything or any action from God.

10. State: *Fortunately, the power of the cross provides forgiveness to all who call on Jesus. Confessing our sin to God lets God know that we know we have a problem to work on. While our worship is enhanced by our confessions of sinfulness, we must constantly be reminded that our worship is negated by our words and deeds in daily life that contradict our professions of commitment to Christ.* Lead in prayer that we will live in faithfulness to God as well as profess our faith in God.

NOTES

1. See Deuteronomy 24:17–22.

2. If class attendance is larger than eighteen, form additional groups with duplicate assignments so as to limit group size to six and thus encourage participation.

FOCAL TEXT
Jeremiah 18:1–12; 19:1–15

BACKGROUND
Jeremiah 18:1–17; 19:1—20:6

MAIN IDEA
Ignoring God's message is as foolish as thinking the clay and not the potter is in charge.

QUESTION TO EXPLORE
What leads people to think God's message can be ignored and their own ideas substituted?

TEACHING AIM
To lead adults to state the message of the potter's house and the broken jar and to make application to relating to God today

LESSON THREE
The Folly of Ignoring God

BIBLE COMMENTS

Understanding the Context

The story of the potter and the clay is likely one of the best-known passages from Jeremiah. Chapters 18 and 19 tell stories that are similar to Jesus' use of parables and everyday events to illustrate his teachings.

Through these stories Jeremiah taught the sovereignty of God. He also offered the people hope, but their hope was fading. Because the people refused to hear and to obey, judgment seemed inevitable. It would be devastating.

The reforms that King Josiah had initiated were good—but they did not last. Under King Jehoiakim, apostasy flourished. In fact, the national and religious leaders were complicit in leading the people away from God. With such leadership, what hope did the people have?

As Bible study leaders, we are responsible for learning, living, and sharing the truth of God from Scripture. As was the case with Jeremiah, such truth often conflicts with culture. While we typically do not experience the danger Jeremiah faced from preaching the truth (although in parts of our world preaching the gospel of Jesus Christ is fraught with danger), people often have little interest in hearing.

The folly of ignoring God is evident in these two chapters. How can we help people hear—and obey?

We do not know how much time elapsed between chapters 18 and 19. They seem to be together to emphasize God's sovereignty, the reality of the people's sins, and the approaching judgment.

Interpreting the Scriptures

The Word of God (18:1–4)

18:1–2. "The word which came to Jeremiah" is a repeated theme of these lessons from Jeremiah. The word from God came to Jeremiah, but it was for all the people.

Jeremiah went to "the potter's house." I find it interesting that this revelation did not come through deep theological musings but in an everyday experience of life. Pottery making was familiar to the people. Not everyone made pottery, but all the people likely had a concept of how it was done.

18:3–4. Making pottery is not as easy as an accomplished potter can make it look. Even then, the progress in making the pottery may not suit the potter. In this case, something was not right, and so the potter squeezed the clay back into a lump and began again.

It was such an ordinary, everyday act. For Jeremiah, for Judah, and for us, it had implications beyond its simplicity.

Hope and Warning (18:5–12)

18:5–6. The Lord asked a question and then answered it. God is sovereign. Jeremiah showed that God had complete power over the nations.

18:7–8. In the Book of Jeremiah, the judgment of God seemed harsh. The threatened destruction resulting from that judgment would be total. However, as in the other prophetic warnings of judgment, God showed himself to be a God of patience, mercy, and another chance.

By now, because of its sin, Judah was well on its way to the end when God would "uproot," "pull down," and "destroy" the nation. This message was galling to the religious leaders who considered Judah to be God's chosen people—no matter what Judah did. They greeted with scorn or worse any message to the contrary Jeremiah delivered (Jeremiah 18:18).

On the other hand, in verse 8 Jeremiah described the act of repentance. To repent is to turn from evil. God's grace would extend to a people who would turn from its evil and turn from false gods to the true God. If the nation would repent, then God would not inflict the promised judgment.

God is sovereign. However, in that sovereignty God gives human beings a measure of freedom in determining the course of their spiritual lives. Judah was charting its own course toward destruction. It did not have to be that way.

18:9–12. Malachi 3:6 states, "For I, the LORD, do not change." God's word and God's ways are consistent. But, the Lord is free in himself to adapt to changing situations. Although the people had sinned, if they would repent and return to God, he would not bring the disastrous judgment on them. On the other hand, in Jeremiah 18:10 the Lord said, "If it does evil in My sight by not obeying My voice, then I will think better of the good with which I had promised to bless it."

God is sovereign, but God has given people freedom to make choices that affect eternity. God intended to bring "calamity against" them and yet continued to plead for them to return. This is a remarkable illustration of the compassion and grace of God.

Verse 12 records the choice Judah made and would continue to make. It is also an excellent description of people who are determined to ignore God and continue in their sins.

As Bible study leaders, can we lead our classes to see in the example of Jeremiah something that helps us confront an unbelieving and disinterested culture with the gospel of Jesus Christ? How can we faithfully continue to do so in the face of this disinterest?

Ignoring God (19:1–9)

19:1–2. In one period of apostasy, some of the people sacrificed children to Baal (Jer. 32:35) in the Valley of Ben-Hinnom. As part of his reforms, King Josiah defiled the area in which these sacrifices had occurred as a sign that such actions should never again happen (2 Kings 23:10). The valley became the city dump. Perhaps you recall when many towns had a city dump. There was always smoke and usually a fire burning. Later, the word for the valley, *Gehenna*, would be the New Testament word for *hell*.

We do not know all of the people who were present for Jeremiah's message in Jeremiah 19, and neither do we know the time in relation to chapter 18. It is interesting that the invited group included elders and priests, two groups Jeremiah had criticized. Why would they attend?

19:3. The approaching "calamity" would be of such magnitude as to be hard to imagine. One wonders why the people of Judah, the Southern kingdom, had not learned from the earlier destruction of Israel, the Northern kingdom.[1]

19:4–6. Jeremiah catalogued a list of the sins of the people. Contemporary readers can look at such a list and believe that none of those sins apply to their lives. Such specific sins as burning sacrifices to other gods, filling the place with innocent blood, offering children in sacrifice to Baal—the people in our classes could never imagine doing such things. However, these were representative sins of their day. What constitutes rebellion against God? In what ways do we commit the folly of ignoring God?

19:7–9. The end was near, and it was horrifying.

The Point of No Return (19:10–15)

19:10–11. There is a time when "God's grace gives way to wrath."[2] Unlike the pliable clay that the potter could reshape, here Jeremiah broke a finished pottery jar. The message was clear. The jar could not be repaired and was thrown into the dump.

19:12–14. God had intended Jerusalem and Israel to be his own. But, the continued and progressive sins of the people, and their rejection of God, meant God would reject them. The people continued to presume on God's grace and on their place as his people. Still, they continued to turn away from God, and that brought the disaster.

19:14–15. Jeremiah moved from the dump to the temple. Is there a symbolic message in that progression? He then stood at the center of all that the people considered sacred and safe. There Jeremiah spoke the unthinkable, and he would suffer for his obedience. Just as the pot was broken, so would be the city. It seemed that by now there was nothing the people could do to change this. It was not because God had no mercy. It was because "they have stiffened their necks so as not to heed My words." There was nothing they would do about it except continue in their sinful ways.

Focusing on the Meaning

This is a hard message. In these chapters we see God's grace and God's invitation to return. But, the people would not listen to truth, and they continued to ignore God. In addition, they chose instead to follow false gods.

I know little about making pottery. However, my father was a carpenter, and for twenty years he taught carpentry at my high school. Sometimes, in my high school and college years, I worked for my dad in the summer. I enjoyed working for Dad. He was patient. He was a teacher. And he wanted us to be able to do things.

Like the potter in Jeremiah 18—19, sometimes we would work on a component of a building and discover that it was not quite right. We could take it apart and correct the problem. On the other hand, some structures were so bad they could only be removed in order for something entirely new to take their place.

The potter could refashion the pliable clay to conform it to his will. The broken jar was too damaged to be repaired and was discarded. There is a time to hear and to respond to God's word. There is a time when it is too late.

Two things must happen. We who have God's word must live it and share it. There are many people who do not know what God says and will not unless someone shares it with them.

Then, like the people in Jeremiah's day and every day, they must decide what to do with that information. The Holy Spirit helps us to share. And, the Spirit is the one who enables the people who hear to believe.

The danger of ignoring God is as great today as it was when Jeremiah spoke. The challenge for believers to share God's message can be as daunting. It is, however, a challenge we must accept.

TEACHING PLANS

Teaching Plan—Varied Learning Activities

Connect with Life

1. Provide modeling clay for each person. Have members create something that represents themselves (such as a hobby, work, or

something that makes them happy). Allow five minutes to create this representation. Say: *Introduce yourself by sharing what you made.* (Teacher should make a bowl.) Say that you made a bowl because it is an illustration in this lesson's study. Display the bowl before the class. (Individuals may put their clay away or continue working.)

Guide Bible Study

2. Have a volunteer read Jeremiah 18:1–3. Use *Study Guide* information to present a brief lecture on the importance of pottery in Jeremiah's day, including how pottery was made or *thrown*. Remind the class that Jeremiah didn't think up this illustration but the Lord told Jeremiah to go to the potter's house.

3. Have someone read 18:4. Take the bowl you made, roll it back into a ball, and then re-make the bowl in front of the class. (Allow others to remake their item if they desire.) As you re-make the bowl, say, *The next few verses compare God to the potter, and Israel to the clay.* Invite someone to read Jeremiah 18:5–10. Ask: *What spiritual lessons do you see from these verses?* (Include these answers: God wants us to be like clay in his hands, moldable and ready to be used as God sees fit. Just because we sin, God doesn't discard the clay but remolds it. Being clay, we have a purpose in God's plan. God wants to use us. Unlike clay, God has given individuals free choice. He can't use us if we are not willing. God also has the freedom to change his plan for using us, depending on our actions.)

4. Read Jeremiah 18:11. Say, *God used Jeremiah to warn the Israelites.* Ask: *What leads people to act as if they are in charge, rather than allowing Jesus to lead?* (Allow discussion.) Read verse 12. Ask: *What is the danger of ignoring the warnings of God?* (Allow discussion.)

5. Say: *God issued multiple warnings to the Israelites in chapter 19.* Divide the class into three reading groups. The assignment of each group is to read this chapter silently, watching for their specific assignment.

   Group 1: Find the verses that contain warnings that God through Jeremiah issued to the Israelites.

Group 2: Find the verses that describe the people's sins, the reasons God issued the warnings.

Group 3: Find the actions God called Jeremiah to take to deliver God's warnings.

6. Allow time for reading and discovery. Encourage volunteers from each group to report their findings. (Affirm all participants.) Expected answers:

Group 1: At least nine warnings issued to the Israelites; 19:3, 6, 7, 8, 9, 11, 12, 13, 15.

Group 2: Offenses included worshiping foreign gods, burning human sacrifices to them, burning incense to these gods, being stiff-necked, and not listening to God's instruction. Answers in 19:4, 5, 13, 15.

Group 3: Jeremiah was called to buy a clay jar; go to a specific gate of the city; declare God's warnings; break the purchased jar; deliver a prophetic message; and go to the temple to deliver a final message of warning. Answers in verses 1, 2, 3, 10, 11, 14.

Encourage Application

7. After all reports, dramatically smash the bowl you made. Ask: *What do you think the message to the Israelites was?* (Strong judgment was coming.) Refer to question 3 in the *Study Guide*, "Think of someone you know who is hardened to the things of God or completely closed to the gospel. How did they get to that place? What do you think it would take for them to turn their lives around?" Read it aloud and then lead the class to discuss responses.

8. Refer to and read to the class the Quick Read in the *Study Guide*: "God chooses to create us and works to reshape us to honor him with our lives, but he reserves the right to punish those who ignore him."

Teaching Plan—Lecture and Questions

Before the class session: Find a picture of a potter working at a pottery wheel; find a map of the ancient city of Jerusalem that identifies the various gates and the Valley of Ben Hinnom. (Optional: make copies to hand out.)

Connect with Life

1. Choose a topic of interest to your class (such as parenting, retirement, social security, marriage, work). Ask: *What is the most helpful advice you've ever received on this topic?* (Encourage responses. Teacher should be prepared to share an example).

2. Ask: *What do you think would have happened if you had chosen to ignore that advice?* (Encourage discussion.)

Guide Bible Study

3. Display this study outline adapted from the *Study Guide* on a markerboard:

   Shaping the Clay—The Action (18:1–4)
   Shaping the Clay—The Application (18:5–12)
   Smashing the Clay—The Action (19:1–2, 10)
   Smashing the Clay—The Application (19:3–9, 11–15)

4. State: *God called his prophets to do symbolic acts in order to illustrate his message to his people. God told Jeremiah to go to the potter's house. There Jeremiah was instructed to do two things, both involving pottery.* (If available, refer to the picture of the potter working at the potter's wheel.) Have someone read Jeremiah 18:1–4. Ask: *Has anyone ever seen a potter at work?* (If so, allow them to share what they saw.) Supplement their report with information from the small article, "The Pottery Industry," in the *Study Guide*. Remind the class that the potter often starts over while making pottery if there is a mar in the clay or if it doesn't come out the way the potter wants.

5. Refer to the outline point, "Shaping the Clay: The Application (18:5–12)." Say: *Each of the next two pairs of verses contains a message from God.* Instruct the class to watch for the message in each pair of verses. Enlist volunteers to read two verses at a time: 18:5–6; 18:7–8; 18:9–10; 18:11–12. Ask: *What messages did you hear in each of these pairs of verses?* Encourage responses. (Teacher should supplement answers with information from the *Study Guide* and "Bible Comments" in this *Teaching Guide.*)

6. Say: *In Jeremiah 18:12, Jeremiah and God seemed to know already that the people were not going to repent.* Ask: *What leads people to think God's message can be ignored and their own ideas substituted?* (Encourage discussion.)

7. Refer to the outline point, "Smashing the Clay: The Action (19:1–2, 10)." Read 19:1–2, 10. Ask: *What do you think was the purpose in smashing the clay into pieces?* (Invite responses.) If a map of ancient Jerusalem is available, point out on the map the Valley of Ben Hinnom. Use information in the *Study Guide* and in "Bible Comments" in this *Teaching Guide* to explain the significance of this place.

8. Refer to the outline point, "Smashing the Clay: The Application (19:3–9, 11–15)." Make this assignment: *As we read verses 3–6, listen for the reasons God was so angered.* Invite someone to read Jeremiah 19:3–6. List on a markerboard the sins that angered God.

9. Say: *God, through Jeremiah, issued a number of warnings. As you read the remaining verses of the chapter silently, watch for the warnings.* (Allow time for reading.) State: *Now you should realize why God had Jeremiah smash the jar. These two chapters remind us that God created us and desires to shape us to honor him with our lives. But God also reserves the right to punish those who ignore him.*

Encourage Application

10. Ask: *If God sent Jeremiah to our state/country today, what do you think Jeremiah's message would be? What do you think God would affirm? What would God warn us about?* (Allow discussion.) Ask, *In what ways does God get our attention today?*

11. Close by referring to and sharing the information in the small article, "Have Thine Own Way, Lord," in the *Study Guide.* Then lead the class to read or sing the hymn, "Have Thine Own Way."

NOTES

1. About 100 years earlier, in 722 B.C.
2. James Leo Green, "Jeremiah," *The Broadman Bible Commentary,* vol. 6 (Nashville: Broadman Press, 1971), 109.

FOCAL TEXT
Jeremiah 11:18—12:6;
17:14–18; 20:7–18

BACKGROUND
Jeremiah 11:18—12:6; 15:10–21;
17:14–18; 18:18–23; 20:7–18

MAIN IDEA
As Jeremiah continued to serve God, he complained to God that his agreeing to deliver God's message had resulted in intense hardship for himself.

QUESTION TO EXPLORE
When serving God gets hard, what do you do?

TEACHING AIM
To lead the class to state what Jeremiah's prayers to God can teach us about remaining faithful when serving God gets hard

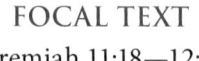

LESSON FOUR
*When Serving
God Is Hard*

BIBLE COMMENTS

Understanding the Context

It was a hard time to be a true prophet. The Scripture passages for this lesson describe that difficulty. In intensely personal, honest prayers, Jeremiah poured himself out to God. Compassion, sorrow, anger, regret, and accusations of betrayal toward God were part of these prayers.

The passages listed in the background Scriptures are sometimes called *the confessions of Jeremiah.* In addition to the emotions just mentioned, in some of the prayers Jeremiah complained mightily about other aspects of his ministry as well.

Jeremiah believed his work was ineffective. It was as if Jeremiah, although fulfilling the call of God on his life, never succeeded. His message alienated the religious leaders and the people. They wanted to kill him. His own family was against him. So difficult was his ministry he regretted he had ever been born. He accused God of deceiving him so he would answer God's call (Jeremiah 20:7).

Perhaps the reason Jeremiah could be so blunt in his prayers was that Jeremiah walked with God. His intimate relationship with the Lord gave him freedom to speak his mind, even when his words were bitter.

Answering God's call to serve and then serving faithfully afterward can be difficult. That difficulty has many faces. People still sometimes threaten and even kill those who proclaim the message of Jesus Christ. In America, that is rarely the case. Still, a culture that is intent on satisfying personal desires and is apathetic toward the church and toward spiritual things makes service to Christ difficult.

Sadly, sometimes churches themselves are apathetic toward their call. Or they can be so caught up in doing good things that they neglect the greatest thing.

The Teaching Aim for this lesson is very important. We study the life, the message, and the work of Jeremiah. Then, we update that story to help people realize that serving God can be hard—but it is worth it.

Interpreting the Scriptures

Whose Side Is God On? (11:18—12:6)

11:18–19. If people do not like the message, they can try to eliminate the messenger. The Lord made Jeremiah aware of a plot on his life.[1] In light of Jeremiah's complaints, did Jeremiah feel that the Lord himself was leading him to the slaughter?

Jeremiah's enemies would eliminate the messenger. They believed that in so doing they could then forget the prophet and his message.

11:20. Jeremiah's confessions shock us with the passion he displayed. He was a righteous man. However, he too could give in to his emotions. When the Bible tells the story of God's servants, it always tells the truth. Oddly, seeing Jeremiah at his wit's end somehow encourages us. God continues to use those who will follow him—flawed though we may be.

11:21–23. Anathoth was Jeremiah's hometown. Some of the opponents likely were from Jeremiah's own family. It is doubly difficult when one's family opposes his or her faith. The sting of their rejection would have been painful to Jeremiah. The year of their punishment was likely 587 B.C., when Babylon defeated Judah.

12:1–4. Whose side is God on? Jeremiah must have wondered with the psalmist why the wicked prosper (see Psalm 73).

The word "case" (Jer. 12:1) is a judicial term. Jeremiah took his argument to the Lord. His complaint was against the religious leaders and customs. He perfectly described the shallow, hypocritical spirituality of those leaders and people, "You [God] are near to their lips / But far from their mind" (12:2).

Jeremiah called for a reversal of his enemies' intent. Where he had felt like "a gentle lamb led to the slaughter" (11:19), he now prayed for God to drag his enemies off "like sheep for the slaughter" (12:3.)

12:5–6. The Lord addressed Jeremiah. Whose side was the Lord on? He was on the side of righteousness. If Jeremiah had a difficult message for Judah, God sometimes had a hard message for his servant.

Was the Lord saying to Jeremiah, *Toughen up*? If Jeremiah could not compete with his peers, how could he endure the even tougher challenges that would surely come?

These verses challenge me. When I sometimes complain, even when life is actually pretty good, what might happen if things were truly difficult? God's promise is that he is for his servants. He will see us through. God will prevail. So will God's faithful people.

Confidence in the Call (17:14–18)

Jeremiah 17:14–18 is the third *confession*. Jeremiah 15:10–21 was the second. In Jeremiah 15:10–21, Jeremiah's complaint was not against his parents. But because of his pain, he regretted his own birth. All of the prophet's efforts on God's behalf and for the people had brought only persecution and enmity.

In Jeremiah 15:19–21, God mildly rebuked Jeremiah and told the prophet he would continue to be his spokesman. If Jeremiah would be faithful to that work, God would give him strength and deliver him from his enemies.

17:14–15. In Jeremiah 15:18, Jeremiah had complained of a "pain" that was "perpetual" and a "wound" that was "incurable." Now he prayed for healing. Serving God is hard. One cannot do it without God.

Jeremiah sometimes cried for vengeance on his enemies and lapsed into discouragement. Still, he was confident God had called him and placed him in the struggle.

Jeremiah faced another difficulty. Jeremiah suffered persecution, and the fulfillment of God's message and the promised judgment was slow to come (17:15). Peter faced the same skepticism in 2 Peter 3:1–9. To this day, unbelief and apathy are huge obstacles to the gospel message.

17:16–17. Whatever Jeremiah faced, God would be his refuge. He could be confident in his call because he was confident in God.

17:18. Jeremiah expected, and at times prayed for, the demise of his enemies. As Christians we might want to hear more forgiveness in Jeremiah's prayers. However, for the prophet the present was what he knew. The idea of an ultimate judgment in the life beyond was not as clear.

Can we see ourselves in Jeremiah? Can we give the forgiveness we wish to see from Jeremiah when confronted with the difficulties he faced?

The Lord Is With Us (20:7–18)

20:7–10. The word translated "deceived" can also be translated *seduced*. This is strong language. God had not "deceived" Jeremiah. In fact, God had warned him, "they will fight against you" (Jer. 1:19). But, in his hurt and his anger, Jeremiah lashed out at God. Are there times when we think similar thoughts but do not voice them?

Even Jeremiah recognized his harsh message seemed always to be, "violence and destruction" (20:8). In return for his efforts he received "reproach and derision" (20:8).

However, Jeremiah could not stop speaking. God's call was too compelling. Paul expressed a similar sentiment when he said, "for woe is me if I do not preach the gospel" (1 Corinthians 9:16b). Jeremiah would proclaim God's message, harsh as it might be, because he was committed to God and to the call of God on his life.

As Jeremiah 20:10 makes clear, that continual ministry would be difficult, even life-threatening. Still, Jeremiah's desire and his compulsion to obey were stronger than the threats of his enemies. This again emphasizes the close relationship between Jeremiah and God. We too would do well to grow in intimacy with God to find greater strength in our calling.

20:11–13. The hope and the promise for Jeremiah was in the words, "But the LORD is with me." Jeremiah further believed that his enemies would utterly fail. In the measure of the culture, Jeremiah failed at every turn. The people did not repent. Judah was not saved. Jeremiah's enemies were able to inflict harm on him. How was it then that he could believe the Lord was with him?

Jeremiah would see God's judgment on the nation come to pass. To know God's call on one's life and to commit oneself to that call is a matter of faith. Results do not always come quickly. In Jeremiah's case, he sometimes wanted God's vengeance to be leveled against the people immediately.

From our New Testament perspective, we know that God wants people to change their ways and to find salvation in following Jesus Christ. If in sharing this message we are sometimes discouraged, we still know that God is with us. Further, we know that our obedience gives glory to God.

20:14–18. These verses represent a second part of this passage. They reiterate and expand the passionate feelings of discouragement, disappointment, and despair that Jeremiah experienced. Verse 18 summarizes these dark thoughts.

Whether or not one has plumbed the depths of despair that Jeremiah described, most of the people in your Bible study class are acquainted with disappointment. Sometimes that disappointment comes in serving the Lord. When it does, we know that we are not the first. The greatest of God's servants experienced it, and they continued faithful.

So must we. Our Father is with us. Our challenge is great. The consequences are eternal. Although serving God is sometimes hard, we must serve because we know that life hangs in the balance.

Focusing on the Meaning

Many years ago, I sensed God's call to the ministry. I had little idea of what that would mean. At the closing hymn of commitment in a worship service, I responded to the invitation the pastor gave. I stood before my home church to tell the people that I believed God was calling me to a Christian vocation.

Sometimes I have been discouraged in my calling—although unlike Jeremiah, no one has threatened my life. Early on, though, I had occasion to wonder whether I had misinterpreted God's call. Then, I remembered that I stood before my church and said, "God has called me." That reality and the knowledge of their (and hundreds of other people's) prayers sustained me in good and in difficult times.

The lessons of Jeremiah are not limited to people in Christian vocations. These lessons are for all believers whose desire is to share Christ and to effect a change in their culture and their day. We face apathy, neglect, disregard for the things of God, and sometimes even antagonism. We must also deal with our own spiritual inertia. However, regardless of the difficulty of serving God, surely we realize its importance.

Serving God is not easy. Jesus said it would not be. But, consider again what is at stake. And, let us consider our calling. Our world, our nation, our neighbors, and our friends include many people who need Christ. Like Jeremiah, our calling is not to be successful as the world counts success. Our calling is to be faithful to the Lord. Our calling is to go and make disciples. Is that easy? Usually not. Is it necessary? Yes, for someone's eternal destiny is at stake.

TEACHING PLANS

Teaching Plan—Varied Learning Activities

Connect with Life

1. Begin by inviting class members to respond aloud to the following *Would you rather* questions. Would you rather:

    a. Clean a kitchen or work on an automobile engine?

    b. Serve as president of the United States or be a professional singer?

    c. Have a tooth pulled or be stung by a wasp?

    d. Give a speech or run a marathon?

    e. Weed a garden or mop a floor?

    After sharing, comment that we get to make some decisions that affect our lives, but often we face difficult circumstances and situations we do not choose.

2. Ask, *Have you ever been denied something or had to give up something—promotion, gift, etc.—because you serve Christ?* Allow time

for responses. Point out that this lesson's study will help equip us to remain faithful, even when serving God gets hard.

Guide Bible Study

3. Use material in the introduction to this lesson in the *Study Guide* and in "Understanding the Context" in this *Teaching Guide* to present a brief background for this lesson's study. Be sure to include some of the circumstances Jeremiah faced and a brief explanation of *the confessions of Jeremiah*. Then call attention to the study outline found in the *Study Guide*:

   (1) A Cry for Justice (11:18–12:6)

   (2) A Cry for Deliverance (17:14–18)

   (3) A Cry for Release (20:7–18)

4. Invite two class members to read Jeremiah 11:18—12:6 aloud, one reading the accusations of Jeremiah (11:18–20; 12:1–4), the other reading the response of God (11:21–23; 12:5–6). Lead class members to form two listening teams to gather details of this conversation, and then record findings on a markerboard. Responses might include:

Jeremiah's Accusations	God's Responses
I was/am like a lamb being led to slaughter.	I know these people from your own hometown are seeking your life.
They continue to devise schemes against me.	I will punish them.
They want to kill me.	None of them shall be left.
They prosper while I suffer.	I will bring disaster on them.
You know my heart is pure.	Things will get worse for you before they get better.
They are destroying your creation.	I am watching over you.

5. Direct class members to the next confession in 17:14–18. You may want to mention and give a brief overview of two additional confessions found in 15:10–21 and 18:18–23 (not in our focal passages). Read 17:14–18, and ask the following questions:

- What did Jeremiah ask of God in verse 14? (healing)
- How did Jeremiah acknowledge God? (praise, 17:14)
- What proof did Jeremiah give of his faithfulness? (I've not run away, and I've kept proclaiming the message. 17:16)
- Did Jeremiah trust God completely for deliverance? Why or why not? (See 17:17.)
- According to verse 18, how deep was Jeremiah's desire for deliverance?
- How difficult do you think it would have been for Jeremiah to trust God? Why?
- To what degree do you think Jeremiah wanted personal vindication, and to what degree might he have wanted God to defend himself? (20:18)

6. Invite participants to consider Jeremiah's cry for release in 20:7–18. Ask members to read the passage silently and select a verse that best represents how they have felt during a difficult time. Comment that in this confession we get a real sense of the inner struggle God's call had created for Jeremiah, and the back and forth battle between his confidence in God and his self-pity. Call on several members to share aloud the verse they selected and their circumstances related to a personal struggle.

7. Comment that when we face difficult times and persecution, a negative option is to become silent on the outside and indifferent on the inside. Read 20:9 aloud, and point out that even in Jeremiah's most difficult times, Jeremiah could not remain silent. In fact, his ability to continue serving God was founded in his calling to serve God. Direct members to Jeremiah 1:4–10 to examine again God's call on Jeremiah's life. Note that our call to serve God is the backdrop for our ability to live for him and our strength to continue to proclaim his message when things get hard.

Encourage Application

8. Ask, *What do Jeremiah's prayers teach us about remaining faithful when things get hard?*

9. Remind class members that Jeremiah wasn't the only biblical character to experience life when serving God got hard. Invite class members to consider the struggles of Noah, Habakkuk, Job, Paul, and others. Emphasize that in every case God was faithful.

10. Comment that we began this study with a game called *Would you rather?* Ask class members to consider one final question, *Would you rather face difficult times and trust God to bring you through, or have a shallow faith that is untested and untried?*

11. Close in prayer, asking for God's presence and power to come into the lives of class members who may be facing difficult times.

Teaching Plan—Lecture and Questions

Connect with Life

1. Ask, *What is the most difficult job or task you have been assigned?* (Be prepared to share your own struggles.)

2. Then comment that while we may be somewhat more familiar with the Apostle Paul's ministry difficulties (shipwreck, snakebite, etc.), in this lesson we are going to explore Jeremiah's difficulties and how he faced them.

3. An alternate opening activity might be to invite class members to share something they have complained about recently (faulty product, poor service, children who did not listen, etc.). Then point out that in this lesson's study we will explore Jeremiah's complaints— what they were, who he talked to about them, and the outcome.

Guide Bible Study

4. Share a brief overview of the previous three lessons, laying the foundation to examine Jeremiah's difficulties. Then ask class members to follow along as a volunteer reads Jeremiah 11:18—12:6 aloud. Then ask the following questions:

    (1) What were some of the injustices Jeremiah faced?

(2) How did he express these difficulties to God?

(3) What kind of response did Jeremiah look for from God when he said, "Let me see Your vengeance on them"?

(4) Do you feel God responded fairly to Jeremiah?

(5) Have you ever felt like a lone voice crying God's message to an uncaring audience or living faithfully when no one else seemed to? (Refer to the example of Elijah in 1 Kings 19.)

5. Read Jeremiah 17:14–18 aloud, and encourage class members to listen for ways this passage is similar to the previous one. Then ask, *How would you summarize this passage in three sentences or less?* Allow time for response.

6. Direct members to the final focal passage in Jeremiah 20:7–18. After inviting a class member to read the passage aloud, ask the following questions for consideration and discussion:

(1) How did Jeremiah feel about himself?

(2) How did Jeremiah feel about God?

(3) What happened to Jeremiah when he tried to be silent?

(4) How did Jeremiah express his continuing difficulty?

(5) What do you think about Jeremiah's praising God in 20:13, but saying, "Cursed be the day when I was born" in 20:14?

7. Call attention to and read the small article, "Why?" in the *Study Guide.* Invite responses.

Encourage Application

8. Suggest the following formula, taken from the life of Jeremiah, for when we face difficulties (invite discussion and response):

a. Check the message (Am I proclaiming the gospel or some other message?)

b. Consecrate the messenger (Am I in a right relationship with God?)

c. Contact the Master (Am I in constant prayer with God?)

9. Point out that we, like Jeremiah, face both internal and external difficulties while serving God. Encourage class members to list some of these difficulties we experience. (Internal difficulties might include such things as feeling empty, feeling disappointed, having wrong priorities, being angry, being busy, etc. External difficulties might include persecution, ridicule, media, general apathy towards God, no one listening, and more.)

10. Ask, *How is our culture like the culture Jeremiah faced?* (Responses might include: we are ungodly, we feel exempt from the word of God, Christians are becoming more reluctant to express their faith publicly, etc.)

11. To further explore our response when things get hard, invite class members to respond to the following true or false statements:

    a. You are responsible for faithful service, not for results.

    b. A prophet is without honor among his or her own people.

    c. Even God's followers have a tendency to shoot the messenger rather than heed the message.

    d. Difficulties are not a sign of a lack of faith but are the most fertile soil in which faith can grow.

    e. Life is not fair for followers of Christ.

    f. Questioning God demonstrates weak faith.

    Invite comments about answers.

12. To conclude the session, invite participants to respond aloud to questions two ("What is your first response when serving God gets difficult?") and four ("How do you feel about the idea of questioning or even challenging God?") in the *Study Guide*. Then ask them to silently ponder question three ("When was the last time God's word felt like a fire in your heart, a message you just had to share?"). Close in prayer, asking God to become real, afresh and anew, to every member.

NOTES

1. "Like a gentle lamb led to the slaughter" is reminiscent of Isaiah's prophecy (Isaiah 53:7). Philip later understood this statement in Isaiah to describe Jesus (Acts 8:32–33).

FOCAL TEXT
Jeremiah 36

BACKGROUND
Jeremiah 36

MAIN IDEA
God's message overcomes
all attempts to destroy it.

QUESTION TO EXPLORE
In what futile ways do
people attempt to destroy
God's message?

TEACHING AIM
To lead adults to state
implications of King
Jehoiakim's futile attempt
to destroy God's message

LESSON FIVE
*No Stopping
God's Message*

BIBLE COMMENTS

Understanding the Context

Jeremiah's temple sermon appears in chapters 7 and 26 of the Book of Jeremiah, but Baruch's mission to the temple, which immediately follows the sermon chronologically, does not appear until chapter 36. A person could name the chapter *Jeremiah's condemnation of Jehoiakim's rebellion*.

Jeremiah 36 is one of the most important chapters in the Book of Jeremiah. This chapter is the only source in the Old Testament that shows how a prophet's oral message became a written message. The chapter also reveals the close relationship between Jeremiah and the scribe Baruch.[1]

The chapter has two themes: God's word and Judah's response. The section reveals that Judah's opportunity to repent had passed. King Jehoiakim's futile attempt to destroy God's message sealed Judah's fate.

Interpreting the Scriptures

The Command to Write the Messages on a Scroll (36:1–3)

36:1. "The fourth year of King Jehoiakim" was 605 B.C. This was the year that Babylon became supreme in the ancient Near East. The following year, Baruch read the message "in the house of the LORD" (Jeremiah 36:10). Jeremiah had been ministering for more than twenty years.

36:2. *Yahweh* instructed Jeremiah to write on a scroll every message he had given the prophet since the prophet began his ministry up to the present, that is, 627–605 B.C.

Writers used either papyrus or leather sheets sewn together, with the writing placed in columns. Jeremiah's scroll probably used papyrus since the king burned the scroll, as noted in 36:23. A typical scroll measured thirty feet by ten inches and used wooden rollers to roll it from one side to the other during readings.

Written messages may have made a more profound impact on the audience than impromptu speeches. Scholars debate what portions of the message Jeremiah dictated from memory or produced from his notes. It is also unclear what parts of the Book of Jeremiah comprised the scroll mentioned in this chapter. Not every section of the present Book of Jeremiah was included in the scroll (see Jer. 36:32).

Baruch Commanded to Write the Scroll (36:4–7)

36:4. Baruch's name is from the Hebrew word meaning *blessed*. He was a scribe and person of high standing.

36:5. Jeremiah informed Baruch that he was prevented from entering the "house of the LORD." Jeremiah might have been ritually unclean and not able to enter the temple. More likely, the temple officials might have viewed Jeremiah as a troublemaker and prohibited him from going to the temple.

36:6. In the fifth year of Jehoiakim (604 B.C.), Jeremiah instructed Baruch to go to the temple in his place on a fast day and to read from the scroll to the people present. The text does not explain the lapse in time from the writing of the scroll to this event. The nature of the particular fast day is unknown. A fast may have been called because of the Babylonian threat against Jerusalem or the Babylonian capture of Ashkelon (see on 36:9).

36:7. The expression "it may be" means *perhaps* and indicates that there was a chance to stay the wrath of God. However, there was no guarantee that a fast would delay or postpone divine punishment.

The Public Reading of the Scroll at the Temple (36:8–10)

36:8. Baruch carefully carried out Jeremiah's directives and went to the temple.

36:9. The verse focuses on "a fast before the LORD." The date was possibly November or December 604 B.C. Baruch waited for the appropriate fast day to go to the temple. The Babylonians captured the city of Ashkelon in December 604, which might have led to the fast in Jerusalem. The people failed to see the incompatibility of the thought that having a national day of fasting would secure God's deliverance when the nation continued its disobedience against God.

36:10. Baruch read the scroll to the people, apparently in a location where the people in the courtyard could see and hear him. The text does not record their reaction to the message of Jeremiah's scroll.

Reading the Scroll Before the Officials (36:11–19)

36:11–12. Micaiah, "son of Gemariah, son of Shaphan," immediately reported the situation to the cabinet officials gathered in the secretary's room in the royal palace. Five officials are named. "Elishama the secretary" might have been of royal descent. "Delaiah son of Shemaiah" is unknown outside of this chapter. "Elnathan son of Achbor" might have been the king's father-in-law. Achbor had participated in the discovery of the scroll during the reign of Josiah (2 Kings 22:12). It appears that Elnathan was no longer a supporter of the king. "Gemariah son of Shaphan" is unknown other than that his father participated in the discovery of the scroll during the reign of Josiah (2 Kgs. 22:12). "Zedekiah son of Hananiah" is also unknown outside of this chapter. It is unclear whether he was the son of the man named Hananiah who confronted Jeremiah as presented in Jeremiah 28:1–17.

36:13–15. Verses 13–21 describe the immediate consequences from reading the scroll. Following Micaiah's report of the scroll, the officials sent Jehudi to Baruch to summon Baruch to appear before them with the scroll.

Jehudi's ancestry is traced for three generations. Nothing is known of his family, although the name "Cushi" means *Ethiopian* and may indicate that his family was from Ethiopia.

Jehudi brought Baruch to the assembly. Baruch sat down and read the scroll to the officials. The officials appear to have received Baruch courteously. They used the Hebrew expression *please* in their request for Baruch to sit and read.

36:16–17. The officials expressed fear, dread, as Baruch read the scroll. Jeremiah's message struck a chord this time because they must have heard Jeremiah's messages in the previous years. They had no choice but to report the message to the king, not as troublemakers, but because they had a solemn duty to report important messages to the king. They apparently recognized the divine authority in Jeremiah's prophecy.

36:18. Baruch acknowledged that Jeremiah had "dictated" all of the words" or, literally, *he read from his mouth*. Baruch simply wrote the messages on the scroll in ink. This is the only mention of "ink" in the Old Testament. We see Baruch's courage in his willingness to admit that he participated in producing the scroll.

36:19. The officials recognized the danger the contents in the scroll had for Jeremiah and Baruch. In anticipation of the king's response, which they knew well, the officials urged Jeremiah and Baruch to hide. The fear for Jeremiah and Baruch was well founded. These officials were probably sympathetic to the content of the scroll, which is why they were willing to assist Jeremiah and Baruch.

Reading the Scroll to the King (36:20–26)

36:20–22. The officials stored the scroll for safekeeping in the room of "Elishama the secretary" and "reported all the words to the king." They knew that the king would respond negatively to the message contained in the scroll. The king sent Jehudi to retrieve the scroll. Jehudi read the scroll to the king and the officials assembled. The "ninth month" indicates December. The king was in his winter apartment, probably the first floor, with a fire pot in the center of the room to heat the room.

36:23–26. The king responded negatively. Jehudi read three or four columns of the scroll and, either the king or Jehudi at the king's order cut the scroll with a scribe's knife and tossed the pieces into the fire pot until the entire scroll perished in the fire. The king, known for his arrogance, might have destroyed the scroll himself. The irony is that the king destroyed the scroll with a tool used to create a scroll.

The destruction of the scroll showed the king's contempt for Jeremiah and the message. The king might also have believed he was nullifying the power of the prophecy by destroying the scroll.

Neither the king nor his officials were "alarmed" concerning the destruction of the prophecy. They refused to tear their clothes as they heard the words read from the scroll. Tearing their clothes was a traditional gesture of mourning. In contrast, King Josiah had torn his garments when he heard the words from the Book of the Law that his men discovered in his day (2 Kings 22:11). Josiah was humble. Jehoiakim was arrogant.

There are less dramatic ways of rejecting God's word today. People ignore it. They ridicule it. They interpret it so as to deny its authority. Rejection of God's message led to judgment on Jehoiakim and his people at that time. Today, those who reject God's message will face divine consequences.

Rewriting the Destroyed Scroll (36:27–32)

36:27. "The word of the Lord" cannot be silenced. The Lord gave new instructions to Jeremiah following the destruction of the original scroll. The verse uses the expression "the words that Baruch wrote at Jeremiah's dictation" and indicates the work of both men on the scroll.

36:28. The writing of "the former words" on "another scroll" parallels the rewriting of the Ten Commandments on the tablets that Moses smashed.

36:29–31. The Lord gave Jeremiah an additional message for the king who had criticized the original prophecy concerning the destruction of the land and its inhabitants. Jehoiakim would have no heir to rule after him. In fact, his son Jehoiachin did succeed him, but Jehoiachin ruled for only three months before the Babylonians removed him from the throne and appointed his uncle Zedekiah to the throne. Therefore, Jeremiah's prophecy came to fruition because succession through Jehoiakim's children ended.

The fate of Jehoiakim is uncertain. Jeremiah 22:18–19 implies that the enemy would drag Jehoiakim's corpse outside the city gates like a donkey (considered an unclean animal). Second Kings 24:6 states that Jehoiakim "slept with his ancestors," that is, died peacefully. Second Chronicles 36:5–8 says that Nebuchadnezzar bound Jehoiakim and carried him to Babylon. Some have speculated in light of these verses that the people assassinated Jehoiakim, hoping to appease the advancing Babylonian army. The mystery remains.

Whatever specifically happened to King Jehoiakim, the passage serves as a reminder that the Lord will hold leaders accountable for their actions. Additionally, those who follow immoral leadership will also be held accountable.

36:32. The chapter ends with the rewriting of the scroll by Baruch as Jeremiah dictated. However, the scroll was not an exact duplicate of the first scroll. Either Jeremiah or Baruch added "many similar words" to the original message. Therefore, there is good reason to argue that the expanded version of the scroll included messages that are now embedded in Jeremiah 1—25.

Focusing on the Meaning

Jeremiah 36 begins and ends with a command for Jeremiah to record the Lord's message on a scroll. Although the king sought to destroy the prophetic word, the prophetic word survived in the end. The events described in the chapter remind the reader that the word of God remains forever. Throughout history, many individuals have attempted to deny it, ban it, truncate it, or eradicate it. All of these attempts failed. The divine word cannot be destroyed.

The passage also serves as a reminder that many have risked their safety to preserve and proclaim the word of God. Others paid a high price to make Scripture more accessible to individuals. Some have lost their lives in order to preserve the word of God.

John Wycliffe, a dissident in the Roman Catholic Church in the late fourteenth century, translated portions of the New Testament from the Latin Vulgate into the vernacular English so that those who read English could read the Bible for themselves. The church declared him a heretic. Following his death, the church exhumed his corpse and scattered the burned ashes in a river. The church council then ordered the burning of all copies of his English translation. Likewise, John Huss, a Czech reformer in the early fifteenth century and influenced by Wycliffe, was burned at the stake for following his understanding of the Scriptures.

By the early sixteenth century, possession of any unauthorized translation of the Scriptures in English could result in a death sentence. Early in the sixteenth century, William Tyndale began what became the first English translation of the Bible from the Hebrew and Greek. He was arrested in 1535, convicted of heresy, strangled, and burned at the stake.

How sad that we fail to read the Scriptures today or, even worse, to ignore their teachings.

TEACHING PLANS

Teaching Plan—Varied Learning Activities

Connect with Life

1. Give each participant a pen and piece of paper, and ask participants to write the words that you will dictate to them. Then read Jeremiah 36:27–28, repeating as necessary to allow time for pupils to write the two verses.

2. Ask, *How would you feel if you were instructed by God to write his words and commands? What kind of task would it be?*

3. Comment that in this lesson's study, Jeremiah wrote God's words not once but a second time after the king burned the first copy. Point out that unlike a phone message that can be deleted with the touch of a button, God's message overcomes all attempts to destroy it.

Guide Bible Study

4. Introduce a previously enlisted class member who will portray the character of Baruch and share the overall message of Jeremiah 36 from his perspective. Baruch may choose to share a monologue, use an interview format, or even welcome questions from the class.

5. As Baruch concludes the presentation, state that since God's message calls for repentance, restoration, and relationship, it is timeless. Point out that this passage is unique in the Old Testament in that it is the only one that directly shows the way a prophet's oral message reached its written form.

6. Invite class members (as individuals or teams of two or three people each) to scan Jeremiah 36 and suggest a simple outline for the chapter. Invite participants to jot the outline on a markerboard. Suggestions for the outline might include:
   • God's command to write
   • Baruch is enlisted to help
   • Baruch reads the scroll during a community fast
   • Officials report to the king
   • Officials encourage Baruch and Jeremiah to hide
   • The message is presented to the king
   • The king burns the scroll
   • God pronounces judgment
   • Jeremiah and Baruch rewrite the scroll

7. Remind class members that the written word of God is the best commentary on itself. To better comprehend the significance and power of God's written message, form two or more groups (as class size allows)[2] and assign two or three of the following passages to each group: Joshua 1:8; Proverbs 30:5–6; Isaiah 55:11; 1 Thessalonians 2:13; 2 Timothy 3:16; Hebrews 4:12.

   Allow several minutes for group members to explore what their assigned passages say about the written word of God. Then have them share their findings with the large group.

8. Comment that neglecting God's word was, and is, a continual problem for God's people. Direct class members to 2 Kings 22:8–13 to observe how Jehoiakim's father, King Josiah, responded when

confronted with the reading of God's word. Ask members to consider the following questions:

- The first time you heard God's message, did you respond more like King Josiah or King Jehoiakim?
- What is God's ultimate desire for people who encounter his word?
- What has God done to ensure that all who hear his message can have a restored relationship with him?

9. Read aloud the following thought from the *Study Guide*: "Those who have burned Bibles or imprisoned and killed God's messengers have missed the fact that God's message is far more than words on pages or words spoken by human voices. God's message is living and active, and its effectiveness is guided by God's Spirit rather than by the eloquence or ability of any messenger."

Encourage Application

10. Remind class members of the opening activity of writing Jeremiah 36:27–28. Lead them to share any observations they had during the activity. Then point out that many in the class may experience a couple of common difficulties—one, writing can be a challenging task, and two, we often find it hard to listen. Note that God is faithful, and even protective, when he gives his word, spoken or written, to his people. It is God's holy word and thus will stand forever.

11. Invite participants to discuss the four questions near the end of the lesson in the *Study Guide*.

12. Secure several Bibles, New Testaments, or Scripture portions that will be available to class members as they leave. Before dismissing in prayer, encourage members to pick up a copy and share it with someone this coming week. Invite them to email you or the class when they have had the opportunity to share God's word. As you have opportunity to interact during the week, remind class members that God's message overcomes all attempts to destroy it.

Teaching Plan—Lecture and Questions

Connect with Life

1. Enlist a class member[3] who has been involved in distributing God's word locally or internationally. Invite your guest to share stories of how God's message is changing lives. Then ask, *What is the Bible?* After a few responses, invite members to share how others, perhaps those outside the Christian faith, view the Bible.

2. Another option for connecting with life would be to briefly summarize Edgar Allan Poe's *The Tell-Tale Heart*.[4] Draw a parallel for class members that the word of God is powerful and unstoppable, and even when someone tries to hide it or destroy it, they labor in vain. The word of God should be in our hearts and minds as a metronome is behind the music.

3. Point out that this lesson's study also shows us that not all leaders in Jeremiah's day opposed God's message, but with the king's attempt to destroy God's word, Judah's opportunity to repent had passed. The people were facing dangerous days ahead.

Guide Bible Study

4. Call attention to the lesson outline found in the *Study Guide* (you may want to write the outline on a markerboard):
   a. Attempt to Silence the Messenger (36:1–8)
   b. Attempt to Replace with Ritual (36:9–19)
   c. Attempt to Destroy the Word (36:20–32)

5. Invite a class member to read verses 1–8 aloud. Then ask:
   a. What is the significance of "the fourth year"? (Be ready to provide additional information from the *Study Guide* and/or "Bible Comments" in this *Teaching Guide*.)
   a. What were God's directions to Jeremiah?
   b. Why do you think God wanted his words written?
   c. How did Baruch play a part in God's word being recorded?

   d. How did Baruch and Jeremiah respond to God's command?

   e. What can we learn about our role from these two followers?

6. Using material in the *Study Guide* and "Bible Comments" in this *Teaching Guide*, explain Jeremiah 36:9–19, focusing on the leaders' attempt to replace obedience to God's word with ritual. Be sure to comment on the following: the significance of a community fast, continued lack of repentance, a few leaders' willingness to hear, reporting to the king, and hiding Baruch and Jeremiah.

7. Read verses 20–26 and share the following questions for discussion:

   a. How could the king have responded to God's written word?

   b. Why did the king respond the way he did?

   c. What is the significance of verse 24?

   d. How does verse 24 compare to the response of Josiah in 2 Kings 22:8–13?

   e. What was the king's order for Jeremiah and Baruch?

8. Point out that not only did King Jehoiakim seek to destroy God's message but he also tried to destroy God's messengers. Read verses 27–32, and ask: *What was God's response and judgment on King Jehoiakim?*

Encourage Application

9. Note that these verses give the reader insight into the transition from oral tradition to the written word. Ironically, the king's refusal to hear the word led to the word being written, and thus even more people would have access to the word. Invite class members to consider Paul's statement in Philippians 1:12–14 and to draw parallels with the focal passage.

10. Comment that some years ago, this bumper sticker was popular: "God said it, I believe it, and that settles it!" Ask class members to what degree they agree with the statement. Then comment that the real truth of the statement is found in the first and last phrases, the middle is unnecessary. Our culture believes it has the right to manipulate God's word (truth) simply by choosing to change it or

not believe it. But the absolute truth is that it is God's word, regardless of people's acceptance of it.

11. Close by asking members to complete this sentence, "I can trust that God's message will always be _____, because _____."

NOTES

1. Unless otherwise indicated, all Scripture quotations in lessons 5–8 and 11–13 are from the New Revised Standard Version.

2. Groups should be of six or fewer people each.

3. Perhaps a Gideon. Gideons International is a group of people dedicated to sharing God's message through the placement of Scripture. Information can be found at www.gideons.org. (Accessed 9/24/13.) Testimonies and stories are also available on this website and can be used if a speaker is not available for your class.

4. See http://xroads.virginia.edu/~hyper/poe/telltale.html. Accessed 9/24/13.

FOCAL TEXT
Jeremiah 29:1–14

BACKGROUND
Jeremiah 29

MAIN IDEA
Jeremiah instructed the
people to make the best of
living in Babylon for a long
time, trusting in God to
deliver them in due time.

QUESTION TO EXPLORE
What should we do when we're
not where we want to be?

TEACHING AIM
To lead adults to explain the
meaning of Jeremiah's letter
to the exiles and to state how
it can apply to their lives

LESSON SIX

When You're Not Where You Want to Be

BIBLE COMMENTS

Understanding the Context

Jeremiah 29 contains several of Jeremiah's letters sent to the exiles in Babylon. This chapter is set after Nebuchadnezzar had defeated Judah in 597 B.C., taken many people into exile, and installed Zedekiah as king of Judah. Apparently, the exiles had not made a good-faith effort to adjust to their new surroundings in Babylon. False prophets promised the exiles they would return home soon. This attitude disturbed the prophet Jeremiah and led to several letters written and sent to the exiles. He encouraged them to settle in the land, build houses, plant gardens, and prepare for the long term.

The passage also illustrates conflicts between Jeremiah and the religious leaders. Jeremiah announced that Nebuchadnezzar would roast in a fire the false prophets Ahab and Zedekiah (Jeremiah 29:21–23). Shemaiah, a rebel leader among the exiles in Babylonia, wrote a letter to Zephaniah, the priest in Jerusalem, instructing him to treat Jeremiah as a lunatic (Jer. 29:24–28). Therefore, Jeremiah announced that the Lord would punish Shemaiah for what he did (29:29–32). Jeremiah 24 provides assistance for interpreting Jeremiah 29.

Interpreting the Scriptures

Sending the Letter (29:1–3)

29:1. The exact date of the letter Jeremiah sent from Jerusalem is unknown. A date soon after 597 B.C. is probable. Communication from country to country in the ancient Near East was common.

Jeremiah addressed the letter to several exiles. "The remaining elders" refers to the ones who survived the journey to Babylon or whom Nebuchadnezzar had not executed. The list of deportees also included "the priests, the prophets, and all the people." Jeremiah 52:28 sets the number of exiles at this time at 3,023.

29:2. Jeconiah is the same as Jehoiachin, who ruled for three months before the Babylonians removed him as king and deported him to Babylonia. The "queen mother" is Nehushta, daughter of Elnathan (2 Kings 24:8, 15). The title "queen mother" may indicate her position of authority. She reigned jointly with her son, Jeconiah. "Court officials" is the Hebrew word *eunuchs*, often used to refer to palace officials. Verse 2 adds "the artisans, and the smiths" to those carried into exile.

29:3. This letter was included in what appears to be other materials sent by a delegation from Zedekiah to Nebuchadnezzar. The text provides no explanation for how or why Zedekiah included Jeremiah's correspondence in the mission.

The Instructions in the Letter (29:4–7)

29:4. Jeremiah 29:4–23 begins with special instructions for the exiles (Jer. 29:4–7). Verse 4 contains the salutation of the letter. The first part of the letter includes several important components. First, the letter begins with the messenger formula, "thus says the LORD." The content of the letter is of divine origin, the words of God, as opposed to the false words of other prophets. Second, the prophet referred to the deity as "the LORD of hosts." The term "hosts" means *armies*. God is thus a warrior God. This meant that Yahweh was more powerful than the Babylonians under whose rule the exiles lived. Third, the message was from "the God of Israel." This contrasts to Marduk, which was the patron god of the city of Babylon, and the other gods of the Babylonians. Fourth, the recipients of the message were the exiles, not the people who remained in Jerusalem and Judah. Fifth, the prophet reminded the exiles that *Yahweh* had sent them to Babylonia—"I have sent into exile."

29:5. Jeremiah instructed the exiles living in Babylon to "build houses" and "plant gardens." These instructions indicated that they would remain in Babylon for a long time. It takes time to build houses. It takes longer to prepare gardens from which they would get their food. They must settle in Babylonia.

29:6. Jeremiah instructed the exiles to "take wives," give their sons and daughters in marriage, and expect to have grandchildren while living in

Babylon. Again, this instruction indicated that the exiles would remain in Babylon for a long time. This is reminiscent of the sojourn in Egypt where Israel entered as a small group and emerged as a multitude of people. They were to increase in numbers while in Babylonia. This implies that they would live in Babylonia for more than one generation.

29:7. The exiles who lived in Babylon must "seek the welfare of the city" and its leaders. The letter mentions "welfare" (*shalom* or *peace*) three times in verse 7. The fate of the exiles was tied to the "welfare"—*peace*—of the city. The natural response of the exiles would be to undermine the government of the Babylonians and seek its overthrow. However, if the city of Babylon were at peace, then the exiles would also encounter peace in Babylonia.

Warning to Avoid the False Prophets Who Deceived the People (29:8–9)

29:8. Jeremiah warned the people not to listen to the prophets and diviners who lived among them in exile. The "dreams" of the false prophets represented only conjecture. Their dreams were the dreams they wanted to dream.

29:9. Jeremiah declared that the prophecies of these other prophets in exile were false, and he referred to them as liars. Some of these false prophets might have been among the false prophets fomenting rebellion in Jerusalem in contradiction to the Lord's commands to submit to the Babylonians. They falsely claimed to speak in the name of the Lord. People in distress want to hear positive news and are vulnerable to manipulation by charlatans. Verses 21–32 shed some light on the interpretation of Jeremiah 29:8–9.

Further Warnings, Promises, and Instructions (29:10–14)

29:10. The prophet warned the people that the captivity would last "seventy years." The implication may be seventy *more* years. This lengthy period must pass before the Lord would bring the exiles back to the land of Israel. In fact, nearly three generations would pass before the captives would go home.

The word "visit" can convey judgment; however, in this context, it expresses a positive meaning. The Persians defeated the Babylonians in October 539 B.C., and Cyrus, King of Persia, issued a decree in 538 that permitted captives in Babylonia, including the Jews, to return to their homelands.

29:11. The pronoun "I" is emphatic in both occurrences in this verse. One may understand the emphasis as *I alone*.

The people whom the Babylonians forced to go to Babylonia were confused about the future. They had seen destruction and death. What would the future hold for them? Not only did the Lord know the people's future, but also the Lord had decided those plans. The Lord had planned a future of *peace*—"welfare"—for Israel. The expression "a future with hope" may mean *the future you hope for* or *a future full of hope*.

29:12. The people should call on the Lord in prayer and turn to the Lord alone for help. They must end their rebellion and focus on the Lord. God would hear them when they did. The statement, "I will hear you," means that *Yahweh* would respond to and not ignore their prayers. The Lord's answer to prayer was conditional. Simply crying out to God was not sufficient, contrary to popular belief (then and now). The petitioner must truly "come" to the Lord.

29:13. Verse 13 is one of the great evangelistic passages in the Old Testament. The combined expressions "you will find me" and "I will let you find me" (29:14) belong together. God will take action to assure that those who seek God will find God. There is a condition to this promise—"if you seek me with all your heart."

29:14. The Lord will not hide from those who "come" (29:12) and "search" (29:13) for him. Those who are persistent in seeking God will receive the Lord's rewards. The greatest of the "fortunes" was the Lord's gathering of the Jews from the lands of Babylonia and causing them to return to the land of Israel. Notice that the prophet declared again that it was the Lord who had sent them into exile—"I have driven you . . . sent you into exile." Only the Lord could reverse the divine punishment.

Focusing on the Meaning

How should we handle depressing situations in life? This chapter teaches us to learn to accept our circumstances and to let God have his way. The people in Jeremiah's day witnessed the horrible murders of friends and family members by the pagan Babylonians. They experienced the removal of everything important in their lives. They had been removed from their homes and every form of assurance.

False preachers kept telling them it would all be over soon. In reality, most of the people would spend their final years in Babylon.

The choice was simple. They could spend their last years with the feeling of disappointment or allow the Lord to work a new work in their lives in Babylonia.

It does us no good to have pity parties or to sit around and weep. Certainly, this is a normal reaction to an immediate tragedy. However, one of the first steps in turning tragedy into triumph is to accept the situation. This does not mean that we like the evil circumstance but that we place ourselves into the hands of God, who makes no mistakes.

In every event in life, God's people have a responsibility to seek God. What life does to us depends largely on what life finds in us.

TEACHING PLANS

Teaching Plan—Varied Learning Activities

Connect with Life

1. Display a Monopoly® game board in a prominent place in the classroom. Place the deeds (with the exception of Boardwalk and Park Place) in an envelope and invite class members to select one as they enter the room. Ask them to find their property, meet their neighbors (people with similar deed colors), and talk about the pros and cons of their neighborhood.

2. After all have found a *place to live*, comment that they had little choice about where they lived or who their neighbors would be, and no one was able to live in the nicest neighborhood. Point out that in biblical days, a somewhat similar situation of having no choice and being where you did not want to be, at least for God's people, was called *exile*.

3. Write on a markerboard or poster the question, "What do you do when you are not where you want to be?" Point out that in this lesson's study, God gave instructions to his people who found themselves in exile in Babylon, a place they definitely didn't want to be.

Guide Bible Study

4. Underneath the question on the board, write the following four suggestions (taken from the *Study Guide* outline):
   (1) Look at the Big Picture (29:1–4)
   (2) Bloom Where You Are Planted (29:5–7)
   (3) Refuse to Listen to False Voices (29:8–9)
   (4) Seek God's Face (29:10–14)

5. Lead participants to brainstorm some of the difficulties one might encounter living in a distant land with cultures, beliefs, and ways of life that are different from those at home. Then share information from 2 Kings 24:1–2, the *Study Guide*, and "Bible Comments" in this *Teaching Guide* that explains the events that led to the leading citizens of Jerusalem being taken into exile in Babylon.

6. Comment that one instruction God gave his people in exile was to look at the big picture. Read Jeremiah 29:1–4 aloud, noting that God knew of the exile. Ask:
   • To what degree do you think God is in charge?
   • Why is it so easy to think that God does not realize our specific circumstances?
   • Why is it difficult to trust God when we are not where we want to be?

- Could it be that God places us in places not so we can get out of them but so we may learn what he desires to teach us within the circumstances?

7. Invite a participant to read Jeremiah 29:5–7 aloud, and then encourage members to form teams of two. Give each duo a piece of paper and pencil and ask them to jot down an outline of the verses. Then ask each team to share aloud one part of their outline that seems to speak most clearly to them. After all have shared, call attention to the second suggestion on the markerboard, "Bloom Where You Are Planted (29:5–7)."

8. Comment that while God's voice is clear, our listening to other voices can complicate and distract us from God's plan. You might want to ask two class members to read two different verses, Jeremiah 29:8 and Jeremiah 29:9, at the same time to illustrate this point. Then ask the volunteers to read the verses again, this time one after the other. Comment that God's third mandate was to refuse to listen to false voices. Ask, *How did God express his views about these false prophets?*

9. Call attention to the fourth suggestion on the markerboard, "Seek God's Face (29:10–14)." Read Jeremiah 29:10–14 aloud and note that God desires that all seek him. Ask, *What promises did God give in these verses?* Enlist a volunteer to record responses on a markerboard or poster as class members respond. Note that God told these people they would be in exile for seventy years. Invite teams of two to pair up again and consider, *How would these promises make the difficulty of exile bearable?*

Encourage Application

10. Ask, *In what ways are we in exile? That is, in circumstances that do not seem the best?* Allow time for discussion.

11. Point out that verses 11 and 13 in our focal passage are often quoted. Ask participants to repeat each verse aloud several times, and commit to memorizing at least one of them during the coming week.

12. Close in prayer, thanking God for God's presence and comfort when we are where we do not want to be.

Teaching Plan—Lecture and Questions

Connect with Life

1. Tell of a time when you found yourself in a living situation that was less than ideal (maybe a vacation or mission trip when accommodations were severely lacking). Then invite members to identify times in life when people face living where they do not want to be (such as an older adult forced to share a room in a long-term care facility, a college student unable to study in a loud dorm, a person moving to a new city).

2. Read Jeremiah 29:1–4 aloud, noting that our Bible passage for today was written and delivered to people who found themselves where they didn't want to be.

Guide Bible Study

3. Invite participants to read along as you read verses 4–14 aloud. Use information in the *Study Guide* and "Understanding the Context" in this *Teaching Guide* to explain some specific factors that led to God's people being in exile. Consider including information from the small articles—"Seventy Years" and "Three Centers of Jewish Life"—in the *Study Guide*.

4. Then point out that although these instructions were given to a specific people in a specific time and place, there are some timeless truths that we can gather from this passage.

5. Invite class members to silently scan verses 5–14 to look for these truths that can apply to us today. After a few minutes ask, *What timeless truths do you find in these verses?* As class members respond to your question, be ready to comment on the truths they identify. Note that responses may not be given in the order they appear in the passage.

Timeless truths that your class members may identify (and that you will want to be ready to discuss) may include:

- Sometimes we have to endure the consequences of our behavior.
- Sometimes we have to endure the consequences of previous generations' behavior.
- God expects us to "bloom where we are planted" (to live life to the fullest).
- God wants us to seek the welfare of others around us.
- God wants us to pray to the Lord for the people and situations around us.
- There are always those who distort the word of God.
- God is faithful to carry out his promises.
- God knows the path he sets before us.
- God desires the very best for us.
- God gives us a future.
- God gives us hope.
- God hears our prayers.
- We find God when we seek God with all our heart.
- God is faithful to bring us out of exile—our difficult situations—into his presence.

Encourage Application

6. Refer to the questions near the end of the lesson in the *Study Guide*. Ask questions 1, 2, 3, and 5, allowing time for responses.

7. Close in prayer, thanking God for God's presence and promises for the future.

FOCAL TEXT
Jeremiah 21:1–10; 38:1–6

BACKGROUND
Jeremiah 21:1–10; 37:1—38:28

MAIN IDEA
Faithfulness to God takes
precedence over even patriotic
allegiance to one's country.

QUESTION TO EXPLORE
What place does patriotism
have in the life of a Christian?

TEACHING AIM
To lead the class to state the
meaning of Jeremiah's placing
priority on proclaiming
God's message rather
than on insisting that his
country's actions were right

LESSON SEVEN
When God Is Unpatriotic

BIBLE COMMENTS

Understanding the Context

Jeremiah 21—24 contains four messages to the contemporary leaders of Judah. The prophet delivered the first of the sermons, recorded in Jeremiah 21, in the year 588 B.C. The Babylonian army was camped near Jerusalem.

King Zedekiah of Judah had refused to submit to the Babylonians and pay the required tribute. Rather than trust in the Lord for deliverance, the king placed his hope on assistance from Egypt. When Egypt failed to deliver the king and his country from the hands of the Babylonians, the king turned to the prophet of *Yahweh*, Jeremiah, for guidance. Hoping for a positive word of deliverance, as in times past, the king sought God's assistance as a last resort.

For Zedekiah and his fellow national leaders, national pride came before loyalty to Yahweh. Jeremiah, however, provided the king with dire pronouncements of judgment, which only angered the king. The events of Jeremiah 38 occurred in the same approximate time period, and Jeremiah 38 should be read with Jeremiah 21.

Interpreting the Scriptures

Zedekiah's Inquiry (21:1–3)

Jeremiah 21:1–10 is set in the context of the reign of Zedekiah (Jeremiah 21:1; 597–587 B.C.), the last king of Judah before the destruction by Babylon. The events described in this passage occurred after Jerusalem's defeat by Babylon in 597 B.C. Jeremiah 21 is contemporary with the events described in Jeremiah 37—38. Two of the same people mentioned in Jeremiah 37—38 also appear here, namely Pashur and Zephaniah (Jer. 21:1; 37:3). Therefore, Jeremiah 37—38 also took place during the end of the reign of Zedekiah.

21:1. The king made a request of the prophet. Following the deportation in 597 B.C. of Israelites to Babylonia, Judah became a submissive vassal to the Babylonians for a decade. However, in 588 B.C., King Zedekiah rebelled against the Babylonians. Pharaoh Hophra (Apries) of Egypt supported this rebellion (37:5). Nebuchadnezzar of Babylon sent an army to quash the rebellion and laid siege to the city of Jerusalem.

Zedekiah recalled Jeremiah's warning about an enemy attacking from the north (1:15). The king had routinely ignored the words of the prophet; however, it now appeared that Jeremiah's prophecies were coming to fruition. The king could no longer ignore Jeremiah's words.

Apparently, the Babylonians had repulsed the Egyptians who had supported the Israelites. The Babylonians now advanced a second time against Jerusalem and prepared for a siege.

The king sent two messengers to Jeremiah following Nebuchadnezzar's earlier attack on Jerusalem in 597 B.C. and before the final siege in 588 B.C. Pashhur son of Malchiah and Zephaniah son of Maaseiah both appear to have been priests. These were respectable ambassadors from the king.

Pashhur was an avowed enemy of Jeremiah (38:1–4). Zephaniah was not as hostile to Jeremiah (29:25, 29; 37:3) and was possibly second in rank to the high priest (52:24).

21:2. The king wanted the prophet Jeremiah to "inquire" of the Lord on Judah's behalf. Not only did this mean to ask what would be done but also it meant to seek *Yahweh's* intervention for deliverance from the enemy. They sought a miracle—"perhaps the LORD will perform a wonderful deed." They based this request on the Lord's prior acts of deliverance. Yahweh had delivered Israel in the past, and they expected God to deliver them this time, no matter the circumstances. Their request is like that of a child who cries, *Mommy, make him leave me alone!*

The king and his leaders did not turn to their false prophets on this occasion but to the Lord's prophet. The God of Israel had become their last resort.

"Nebuchadrezzar" is the more common spelling in the Book of Jeremiah for the Babylonian king, Nebuchadnezzar. He was the son of Nabopolassar and commanded the army against Egypt at Carchemish in 605 B.C. and against Judea.

The expression "making war against us" refers to the act of a siege against a walled city like Jerusalem.

21:3. Jeremiah's speech began by instructing the king's representatives to deliver a message to the king.

God's Message (21:4–6)

21:4. The king was the recipient of Jeremiah's message. The message begins with the *messenger formula*—"thus says the LORD." The prophet's answer was not what the king and his advisors wanted to hear. It was the same message of judgment Jeremiah had preached on other occasions. The king and his advisors wanted the weapons used against Jerusalem *turned back*. Jeremiah announced that the Lord would "bring them together into the center of this city." The pronoun "them" refers to either the Babylonians or the weapons. Probably, Jeremiah announced that the weapons the Israelites were using against an enemy outside the walls would now be used as weapons within the city—after the Babylonians had entered the city. The expression may imply that the Babylonians would slay the Israelites with the very weapons the Israelites were using against the Babylonians. The people of Jerusalem had forfeited the privileges of the covenant by their unfaithfulness. Yet, God would always remain the God of Israel, although he destroyed them.

The term "Chaldeans" is another word for the Babylonians. Jeremiah used the word many times in the Book of Jeremiah.

21:5. Rather than delivering Judah, God himself would fight against them. The "I myself" is emphatic in the Lord's speech. It was not the Babylonians who fought against Judah. It was the Lord fighting against Judah through the Babylonians.

The phrase "with outstretched hand and mighty arm, in anger, in fury, and in great wrath" illustrates the intensity of God's anger against Judah. The word "anger" is the same root word for *nose* and suggests God's heavy breathing, as one who is very upset. The word "fury" means *hot*. The word "wrath" means *to be bitter*.

Jerusalem's destruction was going to be complete. This verse enhances the formidable character of God's opposition against Jerusalem.

21:6. Those not killed by the enemy would die of a terrible pestilence or plague. These verses describe the fate of the city as that of a whole burnt offering, totally annihilated. This use of hyperbole emphasized the horrific nature of Jerusalem's destruction. Yet, not all would die, for verse 7 indicates that there would be survivors. Hyperbole was needed because the words *some* or *many* would weaken the emphasis of the passage.

21:7. In verse 7, Jeremiah added a personal word for Zedekiah. The setting of the message was after the fall of Jerusalem, although Jeremiah delivered it before Jerusalem fell.

Anyone who survived the sword of the Babylonians or the plague or famine sent by the Lord would become the prisoners of Nebuchadnezzar. There would be no mercy, pity, or compassion.

The Hebrew text uses the third person ("he"), which indicates that Nebuchadnezzar would show them no mercy. The LXX (the Septuagint, the Greek translation of the Hebrew Bible) uses the first person, which indicates that God was the avenger and would show no mercy. Although the words seem harsh to the modern ear, we must understand God's attitude toward sin and how sin offends God's holiness.

The three-fold statement "Nebuchadrezzar . . . their enemies . . . those who seek their lives" is not a reference to three separate groups. Rather the expressions highlight the complete enmity of the Babylonians toward the inhabitants of Jerusalem.

Jeremiah did not deliver the message in a moment of anger. The Lord, through the prophets, had warned Judah of this fate if the nation failed to repent and return to God. Judah had not heeded the lesson of the Northern kingdom's destruction in 722/721 B.C. at the hands of the Assyrians.

The term "servants" refers to the political and religious leadership and not to the slaves of Zedekiah.

Zedekiah's sons and many of the leaders of Judah died at the hands of Nebuchadnezzar. Zedekiah himself, although not put to a violent death, died in captivity (52:11).

The Way of Life and the Way of Death (21:8–9)

The choice presented to the people by Jeremiah must have sounded like the advice of a traitor.

21:8. Deuteronomy 30:15–20 offered the people a clear choice of life through obedience or death through disobedience. The compassionate Lord gave the inhabitants of Jerusalem a choice—life or death; the choice was theirs. Jeremiah gave the same advice repeatedly on other occasions.

Verses 8–9 do not contradict the previous announcement of no escape from punishment. God offers people clear choices—the way of life or the way of death. The participial form of the verb "setting" suggests a continual offer of a way of escape.

21:9. The people could choose to remain and die. If they chose to remain in the city and to defend it, they would die. Honor to one's country, rather than obedience to the Lord, was in effect a form of dishonor. The destruction of the city was irrevocably determined. Their death would not be pleasant. The "sword" refers to a violent, painful death. "Famine" indicates death by starvation, a slow form of death. "Pestilence" refers to disease that might involve significant pain and suffering before death released the victim.

The people could choose to surrender and live. Surrendering meant survival. What some would view as disloyalty to one's country was in reality honoring God. Obedience to God trumps loyalty to country. The response required by faith does not always appear reasonable.

The expression "shall have their lives as a prize of war" indicates that the people's survival would make them the *booty* or *plunder* of war. Those who surrendered would enjoy a more comfortable life in Babylon than those who remained in Jerusalem.

21:10. The real enemy of Jerusalem was God. The expression, "I have set my face against this city for evil and not for good," was the opposite of what the people wanted. They wanted God to look upon them for the purpose of saving them from the hands of the Babylonians. The statement "he shall burn it with fire" refers to the Babylonian king as *Yahweh's* agent of punishment.

Jeremiah's Confinement in a Cistern (38:1–28)

These events possibly occurred toward the end of the reign of Zedekiah and should be read with Jeremiah 21. There are several similarities between Jeremiah 37:11–21 and Jeremiah 38. The passages may contain parallel accounts of the same event. Jeremiah was arrested and imprisoned. Jeremiah was confined in the house of Jonathan (37:15; 38:26). Jeremiah met in a secret meeting with Zedekiah in which the content of the prophet's message was essentially the same in both passages. Both accounts conclude with Jeremiah's confinement in the court of the guard (37:21—38:28).

However, several differences exist between the two passages. These include the occasion for the arrest, the specific location of Jeremiah's imprisonment, and the details of Jeremiah's rescue from the cistern (which is not mentioned in Jer. 37). Evidence is not sufficient to support one interpretation to the exclusion of the other.

The Demand for Jeremiah's Punishment (38:1–6)

Jeremiah's messages were still reaching the people through individuals permitted to visit him while he was confined in the court of the guard.

38:1–4. Verse 1 lists several national loyalists who were the enemies of Jeremiah, including Pashhur, who put Jeremiah in stocks. The four men mentioned in this verse wanted Jeremiah put to death because the prophet continued to warn the people that they would die by sword, famine, or plague. Jeremiah frequently mentions this triad of punishment. The four men viewed Jeremiah's message as treasonous.

Verse 2 begins with the *messenger formula*, "thus says the LORD." In verse 4, the leaders expressed concern for the well-being of the citizens of the city of Jerusalem. They viewed Jeremiah as fomenting rebellion and instilling fear in the hearts of the inhabitants of the city. Jeremiah's words were hurting the war effort. They accused Jeremiah of not seeking the "welfare" of the city and of seeking to harm the people. The term for "welfare" is the Hebrew word *shalom*, meaning *peace*. However, the reality was the reverse. What the leaders wanted for the city was not what was best for the inhabitants.

38:5. Zedekiah vacillated as a leader, revealing his weak character as a ruler. He sought to relieve himself of any responsibility concerning Jeremiah's fate. He claimed that he was too weak to oppose his advisors. However, he later acted unilaterally to countermand their deed.

Zedekiah may have wanted to do the right thing, but he did not have the courage to stand up to Jeremiah's enemies.

38:6. The enemies placed Jeremiah in a cistern in the courtyard of Malkijah, the king's son. Cisterns collected water and were dug out of limestone rock. They varied in depth and had a narrow opening at the top that could be covered. Jeremiah 37:15 refers to a confinement in the cistern in the house of Jonathan. Apparently, there were at least two imprisonments. All that remained at the bottom of the cistern was mud, into which Jeremiah sank. They left him there to die. The texts do not explain why they placed Jeremiah in a cistern to die rather than execute him on the spot. Perhaps they wanted him to suffer. More likely, though, perhaps superstitiously they were reluctant to kill a prophet or shed innocent blood, which was an especially abhorrent sin (see Deuteronomy 19:10, 13; 21:8; Jonah 1:14). Jeremiah certainly paid the price for his faithfulness to the Lord.

Focusing on the Meaning

God's people need to realize that sometimes God chastises a nation just as God chastises individuals. Unfortunately, it is difficult to determine when God brings correction on the individual or nation and when they bring trouble on themselves because of poor decisions. Therefore, the only sane response to these difficult times in life is to submit to the will of God.

Hebrews 12:9 reminds us, "Moreover, we had human parents to discipline us, and we respected them. Should we not be even more willing to be subject to the Father of spirits and live?" The implication is that we might not live if we fail to submit.

The "Egypt" to which we turn for assistance today may include our wealth, our education, our network of colleagues, and similar things. We may view ourselves as unconquerable because we can explain so many things that happen. Often it is only when all else fails that we turn to God.

TEACHING PLANS

Teaching Plan—Varied Learning Activities

Connect with Life

1. As learners arrive, make sure they have copies of the Scripture for this lesson. Once learners are gathered, state that this lesson rides on the assumption that loyalty to God is a higher priority than loyalty to country. Invite comments about whether they agree or disagree with that premise. Allow time for as many to share as possible, and ask whether there are any exceptions to the answers given.

2. Display and refer to the following outline from the *Study Guide* so your students can see where the lesson is going:
   - Seeking God When It's Too Late (21:1–2)
   - God Fights Against Jerusalem (21:3–7)
   - Surrender or Die (21:8–10)
   - The High Price of Truth-Telling (38:1–6)

   Set the scene by summarizing "Understanding the Context" in this *Teaching Guide.*

Guide Bible Study

3. Move into studying the Bible by creating a *readers' theater.* Assign readers to take on the spoken parts of Jeremiah 21:1–10, with all other parts read by a narrator. If it works in your setting, ask the readers to stand at the front of the class and read in character. You'll need the following readers:
   - Jeremiah
   - Zedekiah
   - The voice of the Lord in Jeremiah's prophecies (could be read by an individual or everyone in unison)
   - Narrator

4. After reading Jeremiah 21:1–10 aloud in the manner indicated in step 3, say, *Judah was presented with two options: Surrender or die. Let's discuss how that same choice is one we sometimes face today. It doesn't necessarily have to do with physical death. Sometimes God gives us the difficult choice between following God's will or a way of our own making. What are some examples of choices like this that we face?*

5. Form groups of pairs or trios, and give each group a page of paper and pen or pencil. Then enlist a volunteer to read Deuteronomy 30:15–20 aloud for the whole group. After the reading, instruct the groups to make a list of similar words, thoughts, or ideas expressed in Deuteronomy 30:15–20 and in Jeremiah 21:8–10.

6. Lead the class to discuss the freedoms we have in making choices about priorities in our lives. Ask: *What do these two passages tell us about the latitude God grants us in our lives? Why is this freedom or latitude important?*

7. Read Jeremiah 38:1–6 aloud or invite a volunteer to do so. Ask students to consider why Jeremiah wound up in the mud. (Possible answers: He told the truth; the prophecy he gave was not welcomed; the city leaders' priorities did not put loyalty to God high enough.)

Encourage Application

8. Lead students to refer to the *Study Guide*, the focal passages, and their own thoughts to come up with a set of steps for making decisions in life when our loyalty to God is tested.

9. Close with a prayer. Offer an opening sentence prayer, and then ask each person who is willing to voice a single word or simple phrase asking God for help with priorities that put loyalty to God high in their lives.

Teaching Plan—Lecture and Questions

Connect with Life

1. Begin class with a current illustration from the news of a region of the world where there is political turmoil and religion is a part of the conflict. State: *This lesson works on the assumption that faithfulness to God takes precedence over everything else, even patriotic allegiance to our nation. We've seen an example of the conflict between faith and country from another nation. Can you think of examples where patriotism and faith come into conflict in our country?*

2. Display the following outline so your students can see where the lesson is going:
   - Seeking God When It's Too Late (21:1–2)
   - God Fights Against Jerusalem (21:3–7)
   - Surrender or Die (21:8–10)
   - The High Price of Truth-Telling (38:1–6)

   Set the scene by summarizing "Understanding the Context" in this *Teaching Guide* and adding insights from "Seeking God When It's Too Late" in the *Study Guide.*

Guide Bible Study

3. Enlist a volunteer to read Jeremiah 21:1–2 or read it aloud yourself. Explain these verses using information in "Bible Comments" in this *Teaching Guide.*

4. Invite a volunteer to read Jeremiah 21:3–7, or read it aloud yourself. State: *The prophecy from Jeremiah was a warning that God was not going to deliver the people of Jerusalem from domination by the Babylonians but would in fact actively fight against them.* Ask: *Why do you think God was doing that? Do you think God had tired of giving warnings that went unheeded? Does God ever reach the point of giving up on us?* Allow time for discussion. Add insights as seems helpful on these verses from the *Study Guide* and from "Bible Comments" in this *Teaching Guide.*

5. Ask the class to read Jeremiah 21:8–10 silently as you read aloud. State, *Difficult choices are a part of the life of any Christian. Jeremiah presented Zedekiah with a "surrender or die" scenario. Although we might not face such dramatic choices, how can Christians discern God's wisdom through difficult choices?* Allow time for learners to formulate answers and for discussion.

6. Read Jeremiah 38:1–6 aloud, or have a volunteer do so. Ask: *What happened to Jeremiah?* (He wound up in the mud of a cistern.) *Why?* (Because he told the truth and the powers that be didn't like what he had to say.) *Is it always costly to tell the truth? Why or why not? In what ways did Jeremiah's critics put patriotism ahead of their loyalty to God? Why did they do that? What interests might they have had in silencing Jeremiah?*

7. Summarize the events that followed in Jeremiah 38, as follows:
    - Ebed-melech, an Ethiopian eunuch in the king's house, appealed to Zedekiah to rescue Jeremiah, which the king endorsed (Jer. 38:7–10).
    - Eded-melech used old clothes and rags to create a harness to pull Jeremiah from the mud (38:11–13).
    - Jeremiah, once rescued, conferred with King Zedekiah yet again and told him the bad news that the Chaldeans would seize and burn the city (38:14–28).

Encourage Application

8. Close by referring to the small article in the *Study Guide* titled, "Checklist for Balancing God and Country." Read each item aloud and ask the class whether they agree or disagree that it is a way to keep our loyalty to God ahead of our loyalty to country.

Jeremiah 31:27–34; 32:1–15

BACKGROUND
Jeremiah 31—32

MAIN IDEA
Even while Judah was facing
further destruction, Jeremiah
proclaimed God's promises
to restore his people.

QUESTION TO EXPLORE
How can we believe things
are going to get better again
when they are still so bad?

TEACHING AIM
To lead adults to describe
how God's message of
hope speaks to them

LESSON EIGHT
God's Promised Restoration

BIBLE COMMENTS

Understanding the Context

Following the Babylonian conquest of Judah, the land of Judah lay in ruins. War, famine, and disease had decimated the land. The exact population remaining in the land is unknown and debated by scholars. In an act of grace, the Lord who had torn the land apart now promised to rebuild the land.

Jeremiah 31 announces the Lord's new covenant with Israel. The chapter proclaims that a restored and reunited Israel would enjoy a new covenant with the Lord. The restoration would involve both a physical and spiritual renewal. Jeremiah 31:1 expresses this theme in a succinct manner: "At that time, says the LORD, I will be the God of all the families of Israel, and they shall be my people." Verses 2–22 address the bright future for the Northern kingdom. Verses 23–26 announce the restoration of the Southern kingdom. Verses 27–40 proclaim coming days in which the Lord would bless Israel and Judah.

Interpreting the Scriptures

31:27. The statement, "The days are surely coming," often expresses the meaning of *soon, but not now* in the prophets. The event might not happen in the immediate future, but it would come to fruition in the not-too-distant future. Additionally, the Lord was the one who makes the pronouncement, thus giving the promise greater authority.

Jeremiah used the metaphor of farming to illustrate the future blessedness. Because of the Babylonian siege of Jerusalem, the land had faced famine. Sowing and reaping were impossible during war. The result of the war was a land devoid of its population, crops, and domestic animals. However, the Lord now promised to sow the land with people and animals.

31:28. Verse 28 reminded the people of what God had instructed in 1:10. The destruction of the land came at the command of God. However, just as the Lord had determined to destroy the land, now the Lord announced divine determination to rebuild. The promise ended with the expression "says the LORD," which made the promise even more authoritative.

31:29–30. Jeremiah repudiated a popular saying. The prophet Ezekiel expressed a similar idea (Ezekiel 18:2–4; lesson ten). Ezekiel also expressed the doctrine of individual responsibility and developed it to a greater extent than Jeremiah.

The popular proverb quoted in verse 29 summarized the self-pity of Judah's exilic community. The people who lived in exile concluded that their punishment was unjust and that God was punishing them for the sins of their parents. They may have interpreted Exodus 20:5–6 out of context. Jeremiah rejected the popular theology that the Lord punishes one person for the sins of another person.

In verse 30, Jeremiah insisted on individual responsibility, as did the exilic prophet Ezekiel (Ezek. 18). Each person would face punishment because of his or her own sin, not the sins of others. God is able to break the continuity between past sins and present or future experiences. Therefore, a new covenant is possible for all.

31:31–32. The prophet again proclaimed, "The days are surely coming." This time the Lord promised a new covenant with Israel and Judah. The term "new covenant" is unknown in the Old Testament outside the Book of Jeremiah. Israel was familiar with covenants. Their history was replete with covenants with God. Covenants were agreements between two or more parties in which obligations were placed on one or both of the parties.

Three types of covenants were known in the ancient Near East. The *suzerainty covenant* involved a treaty between two unequal powers in which the superior party bound the inferior party to the terms of the treaty. The *contract or parity covenant* involved agreements between two equal parties. The *grant or patron covenant* involved an agreement between two parties of unequal power in which the superior party became obligated for the benefit of the weaker party without reciprocal demands.

Although some in Israel understood the need to place God's instructions on their hearts, the nation as a whole had failed repeatedly to honor their covenant with the Lord. A renewal of an old covenant was not what the people needed. Instead, an internal transformation based on the divine provision of complete forgiveness of sin was required. Only the Lord could institute this new covenant. God promised this new covenant in the near future. Jeremiah compared the new covenant with the covenant at Sinai. The substitution would not come immediately, but "the days are [were] surely coming."

The old covenant was superficial, subject to the whims of the people. Sometimes they kept it, and sometimes they broke it. The new covenant, however, would abide permanently.

These verses are among the best known and most important in the Book of Jeremiah. This passage has become central to the Christian interpretation of the Old Testament and has given the name to the early Christian Scriptures—New Testament.

31:33–34. These verses contain five "I will" sayings related to the new covenant. Additionally, the Lord referred to "my" three times in verses 32–34—"My covenant" (NASB; Hebrew of 31:32), "my law," and "my people." these combinations indicate that the Lord took the initiative in this new covenant. We do not initiate the relationship with God. God is the missionary deity who seeks us.

The "new covenant" reminded Israel that *Yahweh* is a God of new beginnings. The Lord never gives up or quits. When Israel demonstrated the inability to relate to the Lord, the Lord provided for a new way to create the divine-human relationship. The "new covenant" reminds us that God not only comes down to us (Philippians 2:6–8) but also lifts us up toward himself (Ephesians 2:5–7).

Verses 33–34 describe the positive outcomes of the new covenant. The manner in which God would mediate the new covenant would be to write on the people's inmost being the divine instructions for their lives. God's people would have a new heart, a new spirit. They would experience regeneration or rebirth.

Knowledge of God is the result of faith rather than instruction. Immediate knowledge is not the goal; transformed attitudes and behavior are the goals. Forgiveness of sin involves the removal of the sin that is in (written on) the heart. All memory of sin is to be erased.

Jerusalem Besieged By the Enemy (32:1–5)

The events of Jeremiah 32:1–15 possibly describe how Jeremiah showed his full trust in God's promise of future blessing and the establishment of a new covenant by purchasing a field even while the city was under siege. The setting for the message was Jeremiah's confinement during the siege of Jerusalem (Jer. 32:1–5).

32:1–2. The tenth year of Zedekiah's reign was 588/587. Nebuchadrezzar (Nebuchadnezzar) began the siege of Jerusalem in Zedekiah's ninth year. Zedekiah had imprisoned Jeremiah in the courtyard of the guard in the royal palace in Judah.

32:3–5. Many of the people, including the king, viewed Jeremiah as a traitor. The prophet called for the people to surrender to the Babylonians. Zedekiah never understood why Jeremiah would prophesy against Jerusalem and its king.

Jeremiah's Purchase of a Field (32:6–15)

32:6–8. The purchase of a field represents another symbolic act performed by Jeremiah. Hanamel, Jeremiah's cousin, came to Jeremiah to ask the prophet to purchase his field as reflected in the law of redemption. Why Hanamel needed to sell the field is not stated. Hanamel was the loser for not holding on to his land that he viewed as worthless.

32:9–12. These verses reflect how business was transacted in ancient Israel. Jeremiah purchased the field for "seventeen shekels of silver." The silver could have been used to purchase food in the city, which was under siege. Therefore, Jeremiah was exercising great faith. Two copies of the agreement were signed and given to Baruch for safekeeping.

32:13–15. Jeremiah instructed Baruch to place both copies of the deed in a clay jar for safekeeping. The clay jar would have then been sealed to ensure the preservation of the contents.

Verse 15 gives the reason for preserving the deeds—"Houses and fields and vineyards shall again be bought in this land." The purchase of the land indicated that the deeds would once again be valid. People would return to the land of Israel.

Focusing on the Meaning

The basis of the new covenant is the work of Jesus Christ on the cross (see 1 Corinthians 11:25). According to Romans 11 and Ephesians 3, the church partakes of Israel's spiritual blessings. All who place their faith in Jesus become participants in the new covenant according to Hebrews 8 and 10 (see Hebrews 8:8–12; 10:16–17).

The old covenant sought to control conduct, but the new covenant changes the character of the individual. Participants in the new covenant love the Lord and seek to love one another. It is not just another renewal. It is a covenant that is new in every way.

The world may laugh at the Christian's investment in the future just as people probably laughed at Jeremiah's purchase of worthless land in the midst of war. However, Jeremiah believed in the future as God had described. So, too, must the Christian not lose sight of the promises of God, even in the midst of troubled times. God will keep the promises and vindicate God's children. We should always refuse to sacrifice the eternal for the temporal.

TEACHING PLANS

Teaching Plan—Varied Learning Activities

Connect with Life

1. Write the statement, "The night is darkest just before dawn," on a markerboard or poster. Invite comments about what the statement means. Be prepared to discuss whether the statement is scientifically true (it's not), and to mention the quip, "The night is always darkest just before it goes pitch black."

   Consider telling a personal story from a time in your life when things looked really dark but you were able to keep faith and stay optimistic. Encourage others to share similar stories. Move to study the passage by saying, *Jeremiah's word of hope about the future came in the midst of a very dark time in Jerusalem. In this lesson we'll explore these passages from Jeremiah and work on how we can believe things are going to get better again when they are still bad.*

Guide Bible Study

2. Set the context for this lesson by summarizing "Understanding the Context" in this *Teaching Guide.* Enlist someone to read Jeremiah 31:27–30. Remind the class that this passage is a dramatic swing from the tone of previous lessons where God's judgment on Israel was harsh and punishing. Ask: *What do you think it was like for people to hear Jeremiah's prophecy in the midst of their suffering and oppression? What might have been their reaction?*

3. Divide the class into small working groups of two or three people each. Give them this topic to discuss: *List and describe the benefits of the covenant described in Jeremiah 31:27–34. Which of these benefits do you enjoy today because of your Christian faith?* (A copy of the instructions is available in "Teaching Resource Items" for this lesson at www.baptistwaypress.org.) Allow four or five minutes to complete the work. Offer assistance as needed, using information on these verses in the *Study Guide* and in "Bible Comments" in this *Teaching Guide.* Invite groups to report their findings to the larger group.

4. While the class is still in small groups, ask them to read Jeremiah 32:1–15 aloud in their small groups, with each person in the small group taking turns reading portions of the passage. After they have finished the reading, ask them to make a list of the details of the real estate transaction. When each group is finished, lead the whole group to discuss these questions: *Why was Jeremiah so precise in recording every detail of the deal? What did this demonstrate to the citizens and to those who heard his word of prophecy about the new covenant?*

Encourage Application

5. State, *Jeremiah's actions in buying the land displayed trust in God's promise for the future.* Refer to and summarize the small article in the *Study Guide* titled, "Tips for Faith in Tough Times." Use the tips to discuss ways in which learners can keep their faith up when times are hard. Lead them to agree or disagree with each of the tips and discuss their answers.

6. Allow a few moments of quiet time to let each person meditate and identify a few of their current concerns in life. Invite each person to pray silently to God, asking for faith to deal with each situation and to trust in God with the outcome. Close with a spoken prayer for the group that expresses your care and concern and asks God to keep each person under his care.

Teaching Plan—Lecture and Questions

Connect with Life

1. Welcome students to class and open with a prayer that includes petitions to God for each person to receive help in dealing with current struggles. Offer thanks to God for being present with Jeremiah through hardship, and ask God to offer the group a vision of the future that encourages and sustains them.

2. Share a story about yourself or someone you know who was able to keep their faith in God despite facing a difficult circumstance. Explain that everyone faces such times in life, and that the promise of this lesson's Bible study is that God's promises offer hope.

Guide Bible Study

3. Set the context for this lesson by summarizing "Understanding the Context" in this *Teaching Guide.* Invite someone to read Jeremiah 31:27–30. Say: *Keep in mind that this passage is a stark reversal from the previous lesson that included God actually fighting against the*

chosen people. In the midst of all this suffering, Jeremiah's prophecy in this chapter was one of hope, and it envisioned a time when God would restore the people and the nation.

4. Read Jeremiah 31:31–34, or enlist a volunteer to do so. Lead the class to discuss the meaning of the word "covenant." Ask: *What are some of the differences between a covenant and a contract?* (Contracts are between two parties with a court or legal system that enforces them. Covenants can be between people and God, people with one another, and between nations, but the distinction in these verses is that God is the one who enforces the covenant.)

5. Use information on Jeremiah 31:31–34 from the *Study Guide* and "Bible Comments" in this *Teaching Guide* to explain the "new covenant." Lead the class to discuss ways in which this covenant in Jeremiah foreshadows Jesus and his work on the cross.

6. Use a markerboard or poster to list the highlights of the "new covenant" in Jeremiah 31:31–34. Take a few moments to show how the benefits of this "new covenant" are related to the Christian life:
   • Better than the covenant coming out of Egypt
   • God's law within each person
   • Will be called God's people
   • Will know God personally
   • Sins forgiven

7. Read Jeremiah 32:1–15 or have a volunteer do so. If time is short, read only verses 6–8. After the reading describe how the purchase of land by Jeremiah was an expression of his commitment and trust in God's future. Be sure to point out how it made little sense to buy land in the midst of the siege and foreign occupation, but Jeremiah did so because he believed completely in the message he had received from God.

Encourage Application

8. Ask: *In what ways are you being called to express faith as Jeremiah did? Is there a way in which your church might be called to express faith in a dramatic way like this?* Allow time for answers.

9. Close with a prayer that includes a petition to God for trust to commit acts of obedience, even when circumstances would suggest we do otherwise.

MAIN IDEA

Through an impressive vision of God, Ezekiel felt himself called to deliver God's message of warning to the exiles in Babylon.

QUESTION TO EXPLORE

What sort of experience with God would you need to have to be convinced that God wanted you to serve him in some challenging way?

TEACHING AIM

To lead adults to state what the manner of God's call to Ezekiel teaches us about God's call to people today

LESSON NINE

Called to Speak God's Message

BIBLE COMMENTS

Understanding the Context

In Judah's most desperate days God sent his most colorful prophet: Ezekiel. Ezekiel's book is filled with bizarre imagery and behavior. So much so that the Jewish Mishnah required that only a "sage who understands his own knowledge" (a teacher competent in Jewish tradition) could comment on it (Mishnah, Hagigah 2:1).[1] A contemporary of Jeremiah, Ezekiel was among the exiles the Babylonians deported to Babylonia with King Jehoiachin in 598 B.C. Scholars sometimes call the Israelites in this deportation *the cream of the crop* because they were nobles and leaders. Ezekiel was in this category because he was a Zadokite priest (Ezekiel 1:3).[2]

These were Judah's most desperate days because the nation stood on the verge of complete annihilation. The Northern kingdom had fallen years before (722 B.C.) to the Assyrians. The Assyrians had deported the Israelites to other nations.

Judah rebelled repeatedly against the Babylonians, provoking King Nebuchadnezzar to besiege Jerusalem. In 598 B.C., King Jehoiachin of Judah surrendered to the Babylonians. The Babylonians took the king, his family, his officials, and other leaders to Babylonia. They left Jehoiachin's uncle Zedekiah to rule Judah (see 2 Kings 24:8–17; 2 Chronicles 36:9–10). This conquest and deportation was the beginning of the end of the nation. A little more than ten years later (586 B.C.), the Babylonians destroyed the temple and Jerusalem.

The Book of Ezekiel falls into two major sections. The first section (Ezek. 1—36) contains scathing prophecies of inescapable judgment and destruction that were about to fall on God's people. The second section (Ezek. 37—48), apparently uttered after Jerusalem's fall, contains words of consolation and hope. Our focal text for this lesson (1:28—3:4) tells about Ezekiel's call to be a prophet. This call set the tone for the prophet's entire ministry.

Interpreting the Scriptures

Introduction (1:1–3)

1:1. Ezekiel begins with an unclear reference to "the thirtieth year." Most likely it refers to the age of the prophet when God commissioned him. Ezekiel was a priest, and priests seem to have started their service at age thirty (Numbers 4:2–3, 22–23, 29–30; but note Num. 8:23–25, which says that they began at age twenty-five) and retired at age 50. Ezekiel's dated prophecies extend from the fifth to the twenty-fifth year of exile (Ezek. 1:2; 40:1), roughly corresponding to the years of a priest's active service.

The Kebar River was a semicircular canal, leaving the Euphrates north of Babylon and continuing for about sixty miles. It passed through the city of Nippur and rejoined the Euphrates south of Warka (biblical Erech).

1:2. The fifth year of the exile of King Jehoiachin was 593 B.C. (2 Kings 24:8–17; 2 Chron. 36:9–10).

1:3. The Hebrew text refers to *the land of the Chaldeans*, which means the same as Babylonia. People attached this name to the land because the Chaldeans, a tribe related to the Arameans, were prominent in Babylonia at the time.

Ezekiel's Inaugural Vision (1:4–28a)

Ezekiel's inaugural vision focused on the image of God's throne chariot (see 1 Chron. 28:18). People have imagined all sorts of strange and exotic origins for this vision, including visits by extraterrestrials. Despite these imaginative efforts, the elements of the vision draw from aspects of the most holy place in God's temple in Jerusalem (see Exod. 25:10–22; 37:1–9; 1 Kings 6). The Lord of Hosts sat enthroned on powerful creatures (1 Samuel 4:4; 2 Samuel 6:2; 1 Chron. 13:6) that Ezekiel later identified as cherubim (Ezek. 10:1). Cherubim are composite creatures, combining the features of humans and animals.

1:4–5a. Wind, cloud, and fire often appear in texts that describe God's manifestation in the world (see Exod. 19; 1 Kings 19:11–12).

1:5b–9. The prophet often used the word "like" to show that he couldn't fully put into words the vision he saw. The fact that the wings of the cherubim touched each other reflected their arrangement on the ark in the temple (see Exod. 25:10–22; 37:1–9).

1:10–11. The living creatures formed a square with their human faces looking outward. Each represented the highest form of life in different areas of God's creation. Humanity, Gods' supreme creation, came first and faced outward. The lion was the king of wild animals, the ox was the highest among domestic animals, and the eagle was the chief of the birds. The four faces could also represent God's attributes of intelligence (human), royalty (lion), strength (ox), and mobility (eagle).

1:12–14. The burning coals may represent the sacrificial altar of the temple (Exod. 27:1–8) or the incense altar (Exod. 30:1–10; 37:25–28). They may also be an image of God's judgment.

1:15–21. The wheels of God's throne chariot intersected with each other, showing that God could move at will in all four directions. The wheels could fly, showing that God wasn't bound to the earth. The eyes on the wheels represented God's all-knowing character.

1:22–24. In Isaiah 6:1–3 the cherubim had three sets of wings—six wings. In Ezekiel's vision, the cherubim had two sets of wings. Revelation 1:15 describes the Lord's voice as the "sound of rushing waters."

1:25–28a. The rainbow recalled God's covenant with creation at the end of the great flood (Genesis 9:8–17).
Ezekiel saw a glorious, all-powerful, all-knowing God who could do whatever God chose. God was present everywhere, even among the exiles in Babylonia, carrying out his purposes of judgment and salvation.

Ezekiel's Call (1:28—3:3)

1:28b. Ezekiel responded to his overwhelming vision by falling prostrate on the ground.

2:1–2. God addressed Ezekiel as "son of man" (literally *son of Adam*) numerous times in the book. The expression means *mortal*. In Daniel 7:13 the expression took on apocalyptic meaning, as it referred to one whom God gave authority to rule the earth. In Ezekiel 2:1, the expression reminded the prophet that although he had seen a spectacular vision of God, he was still mortal. God's Spirit entered him, enabling him to fulfill God's call.

2:3. God's charge that Israel was a stubborn, "rebellious" nation was a constant theme of the Old Testament prophets. Israel's rebellion was nothing new, going far back in its history. The time was ripe for judgment.

2:4–5. The original language describes the people as *hard of face and firm of heart*. They wouldn't be open to the message God would send through the prophet. Instead of the *house of Israel*, it was a "rebellious house."

In the ancient world, kings sent representatives with messages for various people. These messages had personal, business, and diplomatic purposes. "This is what the Sovereign LORD says" is a *messenger formula*, showing Ezekiel's role as the Lord's representative, carrying the Lord's messages.

The Lord made a couple of things clear to Ezekiel from the beginning. First, Ezekiel's messages would come from the Lord. They would carry the Lord's importance and authority. Second, although Ezekiel would faithfully deliver those messages in the authority of the Lord, the Israelites probably wouldn't repent. Faithfulness in delivering the message was more important than receiving a positive response from the people.

2:6–7. When God called Jeremiah (Jeremiah 1:4–8), God also told him not to be afraid. Ezekiel was neither to give in to his natural fears nor to fret about success.

2:8—3:3. In contrast to Israel's behavior, Ezekiel was to obey God. He was to receive the word God gave to him, symbolized by a scroll he would eat. Scrolls usually had writing on only one side. The fact that this scroll had writing on both sides communicates the idea that God's words of "lament and mourning and woe" were lengthy, thorough, and complete (see also Rev. 5:1).

Eating the scroll symbolized that the prophet received God's word into himself. Symbolic actions involving a prophet's mouth were parts of the call experiences of Isaiah (Isa. 6:6–7) and Jeremiah (Jer. 1:9). Although the scroll contained dire words, it tasted sweet in the prophet's mouth. It tasted sweet because it contained God's words (compare Jer. 15:16).

Ezekiel's Mission (3:4–27)

This section shows how God gave Ezekiel his mission and equipped him for it.

3:4–9. God began to prepare Ezekiel by telling him first that his mission was to Israel alone. Second, God told him that Israel wouldn't be receptive to his message. Earlier (Ezek. 2:3–8), God had warned Ezekiel about the people's obstinacy. They would reject him because they rejected the God who sent him.

3:10. God narrowed Ezekiel's mission further by saying that it would be to the Israelites in Babylonia.

3:12–15. God's Spirit lifted up Ezekiel and transported him to the place where he would fulfill his mission. His experience was so overwhelming that he sat stunned for seven days.

3:16–27. God ordained Ezekiel as a watchman, responsible for the lives and moral guidance of his people. Like sentinels placed on city walls to watch for danger (see 2 Sam. 18:24; 2 Kings 9:17), the priests set apart gatekeepers from among themselves to guard the temple (see 1 Chron. 9:17–27; 26:1–19). The idea of the watchman role of the prophet is developed more fully in Ezekiel 33.

Focusing on the Meaning

Ezekiel's strange imagery in these first chapters can be intimidating. We may feel that the Mishnah was right in saying that only "a sage who understands his own knowledge" should teach the book! Yet it helps to remember the old saying, "A picture is worth a thousand words." While most of us use words to teach about God, Ezekiel used dramatic pictures. Ezekiel's dramatic pictures teach us much about God. They show God's glory in the glowing fire, the clear expanse, the cherubim, and other elements. They show God's universal presence in his chariot throne that had four wheels, each wheel a wheel intersecting a wheel, enabling it to move immediately in any direction. These pictures show God's universal knowledge in the eyes that covered the rims of the wheels. They show a God who judges and saves in the fire and flashes of lightning that emanated from the chariot.

This same glorious God who is present everywhere, knows everything, and is all-powerful confronts us as well. We tend to reduce God to a Being we can manage. Yet the true God is the one Ezekiel depicted: a God who is far beyond our greatest imagination, much less our ability to manage.

Although Ezekiel's call was unique, it also teaches us about how God calls us. God doesn't call us all to be prophets, but God does call us all to be faithful to our calling, whatever it may be. He calls us to build our lives on him as Creator and Redeemer of the universe. He calls us to live faithfully to him, regardless of the contexts in which we find ourselves. He calls us to fulfill the ministries he has given us, and to be faithful to him even when we aren't being successful in the ways the world defines success. Ezekiel's call also shows us that when God calls us, God empowers us to fulfill his calling. We minister through the power of the Holy Spirit, just as Ezekiel did.

TEACHING PLANS

Teaching Plan—Varied Learning Activities

Connect with Life

1. In advance of the class session, research Joan of Arc to remind yourself of who she was and what she did (Google "Joan of Arc," if needed; you could enlist a member to give a brief report). Begin the class session by leading the class to recall details from her life by identifying who she was, where she was from, and what role she played in fifteenth-century history. Ask how she came to believe God had commissioned her. Explore how events might have turned out differently if she had clung to her simple existence.

2. Have members recall other figures from world history who claimed to have visions from God or hear heavenly voices. Note that some of these impacted the spread of the gospel, as when Emperor Constantine's heavenly vision compelled him to legalize Christianity throughout the Roman Empire. Other claims, such as the experiences that led Joseph Smith to found Mormonism, resulted in heresies. Transition into Bible study by asking how God reveals himself to believers today, and how we can distinguish God's voice from those in the world.

   Alternate idea to steps 1–2: Refer to and summarize the introduction to the lesson in the *Study Guide* about the *Study Guide* and teaching plan writer's sense of call to foreign missions. Refer also to the Question to Explore and ask participants to keep it in mind as they study God's call to Ezekiel.

Guide Bible Study

3. Enlist volunteers to read the following passages: Exodus 3:1–6; Judges 6:11–23; 1 Samuel 3:3–10; Isaiah 6:1–8; Jeremiah 1:4–10; Acts 9:1–9. Assign one or two of the passages to each small group, and ask each group to identify the elements in each individual's call

experience. Provide pencils and paper for groups to record their findings. Then have groups read Ezekiel 1:22—2:2 and compare Ezekiel's call experience to their assigned passage or passages. Receive reports from the groups.

4. Lead the whole class to discuss how the biblical persons could be sure that their visions or voices truly originated from God himself. Note the reluctance of Moses, Gideon, and Jeremiah. Have the class suggest some possible reasons for their reluctance and discuss God's role in bringing them to obedience. Ask what might have happened in their lives if they had ignored God's call or refused God's commission.

5. Invite a volunteer to read Ezekiel 2:3–8. Have the class listen for God's message that was directed to Israel and for God's message that was personal to Ezekiel. Direct the small groups to discuss the difference between the two messages and how Ezekiel might have felt about them both. Have them suggest reasons Ezekiel might have felt reluctant or worried about carrying out God's instructions. *How did God address those concerns?*

6. Invite another volunteer to read Ezekiel 2:9—3:4. Have the whole class discuss the significance of the scroll, what it represented, and why God instructed Ezekiel to eat it. Ask for possible symbolic interpretations for the scroll's sweet taste. *How would it have tasted if Ezekiel had rejected God's call?*

Encourage Application

7. Have small groups read the small article, "Confirming God's Call," in the *Study Guide* and consider its questions, followed by discussion of questions 3 and 4 in the *Study Guide*. With the entire class back together, invite responses. (A copy of the instructions is provided in "Teaching Resource Items" for this study at www.baptistwaypress.org.)

8. Lead the class to list ideas for increasing sensitivity to the Spirit's voice. Then ask, *How can contemporary Christians learn to distinguish between God's message and the call of the world?* Suggest

that individuals copy the list and use it to guide their thoughts and prayers as they seek to hear God's voice during the coming week.

9. Have people silently consider question 5 in the *Study Guide*. Close the session by having small groups pray together, especially asking for help in understanding and responding to God's call on each of their lives.

Teaching Plan—Lecture and Questions

Connect with Life

1. Ask the class to think how the word *call* is used in everyday speech (such as phone call, call someone a name, an umpire's call, call for the vote in a meeting). List the answers in a column on a markerboard.

2. In a parallel column, record how the word *call* is used in Scripture (such as God called the expanse sky, he shall be called Immanuel, call on the name of the Lord, called to service). Ask the class to compare the terms in the two columns. Discuss the difference between calling *for* something and being called *to* something.

3. Transition into Bible study by noting that God called his prophets to specific work. Ezekiel's job was to carry God's warning to the Hebrew exiles who continued to dishonor him with their attitudes and actions.

Guide Bible Study

4. Introduce the study of the Book of Ezekiel by using information in "A Glimpse of Glory (1:28)" in the lesson in the *Study Guide*; "Not Your Ordinary Prophet" in "Introducing Ezekiel: Visions of God's Truth" in the *Study Guide*; and "Understanding the Context" in this *Teaching Guide*. Explain Ezekiel 1:1–28 briefly, using information in "Bible Comments" in this *Teaching Guide*.

5. Enlist someone to read Ezekiel 1:28—2:2. Ask, *Why might Ezekiel have received such an incredible vision in his call to prophetic ministry?* Discuss the pervading notion among ancient cultures that gods were territorial, and that their power and authority diminished with distance. Living under the dominance of pagan rule in a foreign land, it would have seemed reasonable for the Israelites to conclude that their God's power was compromised. Ask, *How might Ezekiel's vision have reassured him of God's omnipotence?*

6. Invite a volunteer to read Ezekiel 2:3–5. Ask, *What did God mean when he said the Israelites were stubborn and rebellious?* Have members recall examples of rebellion from Hebrew history (see Exod. 32:4, Num. 14; Judges 2:11–13; see also Jer. 7, lesson two). Explain that the exiles in Babylon were struggling with the same hardness of heart toward God because God seemed so far away. Without the temple they could not offer the sacrifices and offerings required by law, and so they forgot about them. The only time they turned to God was when asking to go home.

7. Before the session, prepare placards that each contain one of the following statements: *Do Your Job No Matter What; Don't Be Afraid; Don't Let Discouragement Stop You; Be Faithful and Obedient.* Display the statement cards in random order. Read Ezekiel 2:5–8 one at a time and have the class choose which of the statements best summarizes the intent of each verse. Discuss how these commands might have encouraged Ezekiel to fulfill God's calling.

8. Have a volunteer read Ezekiel 2:9—3:4. Using information in the Study Guide and "Bible Comments" on these verses in this *Teaching Guide*, explain these verses, and discuss God's purpose for having Ezekiel eat the scroll. Ask, *How did Ezekiel's obedience prepare him to speak God's word to the people?*

Encourage Application

9. Refer to and lead the class to discuss questions 1–4 in the *Study Guide.* Encourage members to voice their thoughts in response to the questions. Allow time for silently considering question 5. Referring to the cards from step 7, ask, *How can God's instructions*

to Ezekiel encourage us to listen and respond to God's call? Close the session in prayer.

NOTES

1. The Mishnah is the Jewish collection of the oral laws. The Mishnah was compiled into a document in the second century A.D. Hagigah is one of the tractates in the Mishnah.

2. Unless otherwise indicated, all Scripture quotations in lessons 9 and 10 and the Easter lesson are from the New International Version (1984 edition).

FOCAL TEXT
Ezekiel 18:1–18

BACKGROUND
Ezekiel 18

MAIN IDEA
The present generation in Judah was receiving the consequences of their own actions rather than being able to blame their difficulties on previous generations.

QUESTION TO EXPLORE
In what ways do we blame others for difficulties we have created or rely on others' good actions rather than engaging in our own?

TEACHING AIM
To lead adults to state implications of the teaching of individual responsibility

LESSON TEN
Where Responsibility Lies

BIBLE COMMENTS

Understanding the Context

In lesson nine we explored Ezekiel's inaugural vision and call (Ezekiel 1:1—3:27). In the intervening chapters the prophet pronounced words of unrelenting judgment on Israel. In chapters 4—5 he added symbolic prophecy to spoken prophecy as he dramatized the siege of Jerusalem and all the suffering that accompanied it. In chapter 6 he prophesied against the mountains of Israel, while in chapter 7 he pronounced the end of the nation. Chapters 8—11 describe an extended vision of the prophet in which he was in the holy temple and saw idolatry openly taking place. He also saw the departure of the glory of the Lord from the temple (to be studied in lesson thirteen). The prophet engaged in symbolic prophecy again in chapter 12, depicting the plight of the exiles. In chapters 13—14 Ezekiel condemned false prophets and idolaters. Chapter 15 describes Israel as a useless vine, while chapter 16 focuses on an allegory that depicts God's love and care for Israel despite her unfaithfulness to him. Chapter 17 employs the images of two eagles and a vine to describe the fate of both the people remaining in Jerusalem and the exiles.

All these prophecies surely made a deep impression on the people. They saw the certainty of God's judgment. Nonetheless, like humans of all ages they wanted to avoid responsibility for the bad things that were happening to them. They had some scriptural support for their views. Passages like Exodus 20:5 and Deuteronomy 5:9 said that God punished children for the sins of their fathers. Many of the exiles came to the conclusion that this was the case in their situation. They believed they were innocent and God was unjustly punishing them for the sins of their parents.

The prophet challenged this idea in Ezekiel 18. The result is the first lengthy and well-defined effort in Israelite history to present the idea that a person's individual actions determine his or her fate.

Interpreting the Scriptures

Proverb of Complaint (18:1–2)

This proverb is the central concern of the entire chapter. It reflects the experience of eating grapes that aren't quite ripe. When people do that, they usually have an unpleasant sensation on their teeth. This sensation usually happens to the person who eats the grapes. But this proverb describes the displacement of consequences. It would be absurd for this to happen in the natural world, and it seems equally absurd for God to judge children for their parents' sins.

Ultimately this proverb was a protest against the way God treats his people. Its use in this context questions the idea of inherited guilt that went all the way back to the Ten Commandments (Exod. 20:5; Deut. 5:9). Lamentations 5:7 expresses a similar sentiment. Jeremiah quoted the same proverb (Jeremiah 31:29–30) to talk about individual responsibility in the future.

For Ezekiel the problem with this proverb was that it showed a loss of reverence for God and resentment over the way God runs the world. People believed that punishing children for their parents' sins was incongruent with the idea of a righteous God. In fact it drew into question the whole idea of God's righteousness. Both Jeremiah and Ezekiel saw that this proverb was dangerous because it led to attitudes of fatalism and irresponsibility. It allowed the exiles to free themselves from their responsibility for the judgment they were experiencing.

The Person Who Sins Will Die (18:3–20)

18:3–4. This may be the first challenge in the Old Testament to the idea that God punishes children for the sins of their parents. It's definitely the most extensive. Much of the earlier portions of the Old Testament reflect the concept that people stand together as a tightly-connected organism, not apart as separate individuals. These portions emphasize the community, not the individual. The Book of Ezekiel reflects the growth of the idea of individual accountability and responsibility. This idea may have become more prominent as the nation fell apart.

Verse 4 stresses God's sovereignty. God can do whatever God chooses to do, even hold children responsible for the sins of their parents. He is above human criticism. Yet God chooses to make people responsible for their individual sins. The term used here for "soul" is the Hebrew word *nephesh*. It means *living being*, and refers to the whole person, physical and spiritual, not just the spiritual parts.

18:5–9. Verses 5–19 describe three cases of individual responsibility. The first describes a righteous person who lives according to the principles of the holiness code (see Leviticus 17—26). The prophet began with issues that involve sins against God and moved to sins against people, following the pattern of the Ten Commandments. The first commands listed relate to the true worship of the Lord and the oppression of the poor. It would have been especially tempting to violate these commands during the exile.

Eating at the mountain shrines involved eating meat without properly disposing of the blood (see Lev. 17:1–9). Not worshiping idols meant worshiping God properly (Exod. 20:4–6; Lev. 19:4; Deut. 12:2–4). The law prohibited adultery (Lev. 20:10) and having sexual relations while the woman was menstruating (Lev. 15:19–24). Economic oppression was sinful (Exod. 20:15; Lev. 19:13; Deut. 15:11; 23:19–20). A person could receive a cloak as a pledge for a loan but had to return it if the debtor needed it (Exod. 22:25–27). The fatherless and resident alien were easy targets of oppression (Malachi 3:5).

Although the exiles lived apart from the temple, Ezekiel showed that they were still accountable for the commands God gave their community.

18:10–13. The second example advanced a generation to the son of the righteous man. Despite the good example set by the father before the son, the son disobeyed God. His father's righteousness wouldn't save him. If he sinned, he would die for his sins.

18:14–18. The third example advanced yet another generation to the son of the unrighteous man. If he lived righteously, he wouldn't have to answer for his father's sin. Instead, God would judge him for his own behavior.

18:19–20. Ezekiel's opponents questioned his teaching because it appeared to contradict the law that the Israelites had passed down for generations. It didn't seem to fit the idea of the solidarity of family and nation. The prophet held fast by maintaining again that God holds individuals accountable for their sins and won't judge them for what their predecessors did. (See also Ezek. 14:12–20; Deut. 24:16.)

Repent and Live (18:21–32)

18:21–24. In a fourth example Ezekiel presented another new principle: God will save a wicked person who repents, and God will judge a righteous person who sins. People can be free not only from the sins of their predecessors but also from their own past sins. All they need to do is repent of them. This repentance is more than having sorrow over your sin. It's turning from your sins.

The prophet's main point was that God didn't deal with humanity mechanically. Instead God related to persons and dealt with them personally. He didn't condemn the unrighteous to inevitable judgment. They didn't have to remain as they were. They could turn to God, forsake their sins, and receive God's forgiveness. Conversely, the righteous couldn't presume on God. They always had to be careful to obey God's commands. They couldn't rely on their past righteousness to cover any current or future unrighteousness.

God takes no pleasure in the destruction of the wicked. Instead, God takes pleasure when people forsake their sins, turn to him, and gain life.

18:25–29. The prophet took the people's protest against God and turned it against them. He repeated his arguments to lead them to repentance. They wanted to hide behind their accusation of God's injustice. As long as they could blame their ancestors for the judgment they faced, they didn't have to deal with their own sins. The idea that they were responsible for their own sins was both liberating and demanding. It was liberating because it freed them from the guilt of past generations. It was demanding because it meant that they had to pay close attention to their conduct. They could no longer avoid responsibility by blaming others for their problems. Ultimately *they* were unjust, not God.

18:30–32. These verses echo Ezekiel 11:19 (see also Jer. 31:31–34; 32:36–41). Ezekiel came to the appeal of his message, the way preachers challenge their listeners just before they issue *the invitation*. He called for individual commitment and decision. God's gift of salvation called for a response, to receive the new life God offered. The prophet said that the Israelites needed to do more than conform to the law outwardly. They needed inner spiritual revolution. They needed a new heart and a new spirit. "Heart" and "spirit" referred to essentially the same thing: a person's inner character. God's people needed to get these things from God as his gift.

The prophet ended his appeal with the heartrending question, "Why will you die?" If they died, it would be because of their own decision. It wouldn't be because of God's decree based on the sins of their ancestors. It wouldn't be because of their past sins. They would die because they refused to repent and receive God's gift of salvation.

Focusing on the Meaning

Ever since we humans first sinned, we've tried to avoid responsibility for our actions (see Genesis 3:8–13). The Israelites of Ezekiel's time sought to avoid responsibility for their sins by blaming previous generations. They believed they had done nothing to deserve God's judgment.

God sent Ezekiel with a new teaching. Each person was responsible for his or her own sin. If people experienced judgment, it was because of what they had done, not what their predecessors had done. On the surface, Exodus and Ezekiel seem to be at odds with each other. Yet both spoke the truth. At times children suffer for the sins of their parents. For example, if we ruin our world with pollution to the extent that we can't undo the damage, then our children will live in a harsh and ugly environment. Yet God doesn't directly punish us for our parent's sins. He holds us responsible for what we do. I once heard the great theologian Elton Trueblood say, "All truth contains a measure of paradox." The idea that our children can suffer for our sins and yet that God holds us each responsible for our own sins is an example of paradoxical truth.

Ultimately, Ezekiel's message is good news. It means that we're free. Although we live in the context of the sins of our ancestors, those sins don't control our destinies. God holds us responsible for what we do. Better than that, our own past sins don't control our destinies. If we repent of them, God will forgive us and grant us new life.

Ezekiel also gives us a warning. We can't presume on our parents' righteousness or our past and present righteousness. God saves us by grace through our faith in Christ. We celebrate God's grace and the fresh start God gives us. But at the same time we remember that God's grace calls us not to presume on God's mercy but to live in greater obedience to him.

TEACHING PLANS

Teaching Plan—Varied Learning Activities

Connect with Life

1. Before the session prepare slips of paper with printed phrases such as these: *Cheating on Taxes; Cheating on Diets; Not Turning in Homework; Speeding; Cheating on a Spouse; Shoplifting; Missing a Meeting; Running Late for Class,* or other things for which people make excuses. As the session begins, have individuals take turns pulling slips from a basket or container. Have each person read the chosen phrase silently and make up an excuse to fit the topic (for example, an excuse for speeding might be *I'm late for an appointment).* The class will try to guess what the subject is from the excuse. When they guess correctly, have them suggest two or three alternate excuses people might give for that same wrong choice. (A copy of the printed phrases is available in "Teaching Resource Items" for this study at www.baptistwaypress.org.)

2. Note that the tendency to make excuses begins in childhood. Ask people to think of two or three examples of excuses young children might give for misbehavior, such as, *My friend made me do it.* Discuss why people try to evade responsibility for their choices by making excuses. Transition into Bible study by pointing out that Judah did the same thing in their relationship with God.

Guide Bible Study

3. Enlist a volunteer to read Ezekiel 18:1–2. Explain that this proverb was well-known in several ancient cultures. It would have been familiar to the Babylonians as well as to the Israelites. Discuss the meaning of the proverb, using information in the *Study Guide* and "Bible Comments" on these verses in this *Teaching Guide*. When considering the proverb's symbolic implications, note that the "sour grapes" not only leave a bad taste in the mouth but also cause the stomach to hurt. Ask members to make up alternate proverbs about deferred responsibility using elements that are more contemporary than sour grapes (for example, the fathers cheat on their taxes and the IRS audits their adult children, or turn it around by saying something like an adult child runs a red light and the parent receives a ticket). Ask why the Israelites were applying this type of proverb to their circumstances. Follow by discussing question 1 in the *Study Guide*: "Why did the exiled Israelites have trouble acknowledging their role in earning God's punishment?"

4. Invite someone to read Ezekiel 18:3–4. Discuss God's response. Ask, *What misunderstanding was God trying to correct?* Discuss question 2 in the *Study Guide*: "Why do you think it was important to God that the people understand the truth of their guilt?"

5. Divide the class into three groups.[1] Assign one of the following passages to each group: Ezekiel 18:5–9; 18:10–13; 18:14–17. Have each group study its passage and create a brief written character profile of the person described in it. When all are done, ask groups to share their profiles with the class. In the large group, ask, *What made the men in each of the case studies acceptable or unacceptable to God?* (their individual response to God) Note how actions directly affecting relationship with God were addressed first in each study. Ask, *Why do you think God used these case studies instead of just telling the people what he wanted from them?*

Encourage Application

6. Note that the men in the case studies were judged righteous or unrighteous based on how they kept or disobeyed the

commandments of God's law. Returning to groups, have everyone read John 14:15. Ask the groups to identify observable actions and attitudes among today's Christians that give evidence of righteous or unrighteous lives. Identify factors that may cause believers to fall short of God's standards.

7. Direct the small groups to discuss questions 3–5 in the *Study Guide*, giving special attention to the subject of personal and corporate accountability. Encourage individuals to share with their groups some areas in which they might benefit from greater accountability. Discuss the role of accountability partners in encouraging Christian growth. Close the session by having groups pray together.

Teaching Plan—Lecture and Questions

Connect with Life

1. Share the following case studies:

   A few years ago, a well-known Hollywood actress was caught with more than $5,000 worth of goods she had shoplifted from a pricey department store. She claimed she was innocent because she was researching a movie role.

   After being stopped for speeding, another high-profile actress tried to explain away the cocaine found on her person by claiming that she had borrowed the pants from someone else and put them on without knowing there were drugs in the pocket.

   Discovered consorting with women in a European hotel room, an international political figure claimed that he hadn't recognized the girls as prostitutes because they were all naked.

2. Ask, *Do you believe any of the excuses used by the people in the case studies? Why did those particular excuses prove ineffective in getting those people out of trouble? What is the earliest excuse recorded in the Bible?* (Adam blaming God and Eve, and Eve blaming the serpent after they tasted the forbidden fruit, Gen. 3:12–13). Discuss the human tendency to rationalize or explain away mistakes by making excuses. Transition into Bible study by noting that today's

lesson deals with taking responsibility and accepting consequences for our own choices.

Guide Bible Study

3. Lead the class to explain the meaning of the phrase *pass the buck*. Ask members to think of examples of people who tried to pass the buck. Explain that another term for passing the buck is deferred responsibility—trying to avoid blame by passing it on to someone or something else.

4. Have someone read Ezekiel 18:1–2. Discuss how this proverb describes deferred responsibility. Provide information as seems helpful from the *Study Guide* and "Bible Comments" in this *Teaching Guide*. Ask, *When the exiled Israelites quoted the proverb, what responsibility were they trying to avoid?* Read verses 3–4. Ask, *How do these verses show that the exiles misunderstood God's justice?*

5. Read 18:5–9 one verse at a time. After each verse, have the class think of one word or phrase that summarizes the verse. For example, "He does not eat at the mountain shrines or look to the idols . . ." might be summarized as *faithful* or *God-fearing*. "He does not commit robbery" might equal *honest*. Record the word or phrase summaries on the board under the heading *Righteous*.

6. Go through the next section, Ezekiel 18:10–13, in the same way ("He eats at the mountain shrines" = *idolatry*). Record the line summaries under the heading *Unrighteous*.

7. As the class goes through verses 14–18 line by line in the same manner, put a check mark by any word under the *Righteous* heading that is repeated and add any additional words that are suggested.

Encourage Application

8. Review the terms in the *Righteous* column. Note that the list reflects God's expectations for the Israelites. Ask, *Which of the listed attributes does God expect to see in Christians today?* Discuss what the

attributes might look like when put into practice by contemporary Christians. For example, what would be a modern equivalent for saying, "He does not eat at the mountain shrines."

9. Lead the class in discussing the questions in the *Study Guide*. Close the session with prayer.

NOTES

1. No more than six people per group. Form additional groups and give duplicate assignments if attendance is larger than eighteen.

FOCAL TEXT
Ezekiel 20:1–32

BACKGROUND
Ezekiel 20:1–44

MAIN IDEA

Israel, down to the present generation in Ezekiel, had refused to follow God, rejecting God's gracious actions on their behalf.

QUESTION TO EXPLORE

What is *our* story in relation to God's gracious acts on our behalf?

TEACHING AIM

To lead adults to trace from this Scripture passage God's gracious acts on behalf of Israel and how Israel had rejected them and to identify applications for their lives

LESSON ELEVEN

A History of Rejected Grace

BIBLE COMMENTS

Understanding the Context

In the larger context of the Old Testament story, Ezekiel was not the first prophet to Judah who challenged the sinful rebellion of God's people in an attempt to re-direct them. For example, not long before Ezekiel was called, Jeremiah had lifted his voice to correct Judah, and you studied his messages in lessons one through eight. Even further back, both Micah and Isaiah long ago had confronted Judah's misbehavior—more than 130 years before Ezekiel's call to be a prophet in 593 B.C.

Isaiah ridiculed the empty worship of God's people. Rather than show genuine gratitude for God's gracious blessings, Judah offered empty, legalistic ritual that fooled only themselves but certainly did not hoodwink God. Read the biting sarcasm and repudiation in Isaiah 1, especially verses 10–17 ("Hear the word of the Lord, you rulers of Sodom! Listen to the teaching of our God, you people of Gomorrah! . . . Your new moons and your appointed festivals my soul hates; they have become a burden to me, I am weary of bearing them.").[1] But the people ignored the prophet back then.

Micah had described Judah's blatant misconduct in graphic detail and warned the people about dire future consequences that would result from it. Read the challenging confrontation and chilling prediction in Micah 3, especially verses 9–12 ("Hear this, you rulers . . . and chiefs . . . who build Zion with blood and Jerusalem with wrong! . . . Therefore because of you Zion shall be plowed as a field; Jerusalem shall become a heap of ruins, and the mountain of the house a wooded height."). But the people ignored their prophet back then.

Now came Ezekiel's turn, but the context was quite different. As we sometimes say today, "a lot of water had gone under the bridge" since the days of Isaiah and Micah. And the rushing waters of unchecked rebellion had risen to flood stage by the time of Jeremiah and Ezekiel.

The year was "the seventh year" of the exile of King Jehoiachin, or 591 B.C. (compare Ezekiel 20:1 with Ezek. 1:2 and 8:1). By this date, the Babylonian Exile already had begun—at least for the large group of Judah's leaders, including the priest Ezekiel. They were removed from Judah in the first deportation in 597 B.C. and were taken to the city of Babylon. The temple of Solomon still stood in Jerusalem, although stripped of its priesthood and sacrificial system. But its days were numbered, too. In just four short years after Ezekiel 20:1 (587 B.C.) King Nebuchadrezzar (also spelled Nebuchadnezzar) of Babylon would destroy Jerusalem, slaughter many of the inhabitants, and burn that beloved temple to the ground. Micah's prediction of "a heap of ruins" would become a starkly devastating reality.

How could it have come to this? How did the people of God—born of the seed of Abraham and borne throughout their history by the God of the Exodus and Sinai—come to such a destructive end? Why did they find themselves in God-forsaken Babylon, so far away from their Promised Land and the provision of their Lord?

Interpreting the Scriptures

A Conversation Among the Leaders (20:1–3)

While in Babylon, Ezekiel and his exiled countrymen were under *city arrest.* That is, they could move about their neighborhoods, visiting in the homes of one another, but they could not leave the city and go back home. Imagine a kind of Jewish ghetto or precinct somewhere in the city of Babylon. So the elders among the people of Judah occasionally (see Ezek. 8:1) would seek out their old priest. He now found himself with time on his hands, so far away from his temple duties back in Jerusalem. They discussed among themselves the things of God, seeking from God's spokesman the message God had for them now.

But this particular conversation definitely was not nostalgic—with a shared yearning for the good old days back home. The priest of ritual had become a prophet of righteousness. He lowered the boom of judgment on the sins of Judah's past history of rebellion against God. In a message straight from God (20:2), Ezekiel reviewed their past.

God was saying through Ezekiel (20:3): *Do you leaders really expect me to believe that you are coming here sincerely to ask and seek my will? You've wasted every opportunity to follow my will in the past. You won't be asking me any more questions. It's time for me to tell you a thing or two right here and now!* So God led Ezekiel to make the key point that for generations—from the covenant instructions (*Torah*) at Sinai onward—Judah had not acted consistently with the covenant information they knew so well. They need not ask why they were sitting in exile in Babylon—the answer was as clear as 20–20 hindsight.

The next section, Ezekiel 20:4–32, is Ezekiel's blunt recital of Israel's sordid history.

Rebels Before They Left Egypt (20:4–9)

20:4–7. The review of Judah's long history of failure began at the very beginning. From the time even *before* God led the Israelites out of Egypt, they were worshiping false gods. The faith of their forefathers Abraham, Isaac, and Jacob had been lost in idolatry.

God told them clearly that these idols should be cast aside. God, not the idols, was the One who would act so decisively for them "in bringing them out of the land of Egypt" (20:9). God required their total loyalty and fidelity.

20:8–9. When the people failed to comply, God considered wiping them out completely. But what would all the nations say about a God who expended so much effort—grace—to save a people and then summarily destroyed them? (Moses had used the same reasoning in Exodus 32:11–12 and Numbers 14:13–19.) God expected Israel to be God's "light to the nations" (Isa. 42:6), not to become the reason unbelievers turned away from God.

Rebels in the Wilderness (20:10–26)

20:10–13a. The wilderness is mentioned, but Mount Sinai is not explicitly named. The Sinai Covenant was a high and holy moment—God's gift of "my statutes . . . my ordinances . . . and my sabbaths" to guide the people's life with God and one another. But the mountain-top experience of receiving God's revelation of truth had been swallowed up in the repeated failure of Israel to live up to those divinely-given guidelines.

20:13b–17. Once again, God considered wiping out the entire rebellious people and never bringing them all the way from Egypt to the Promised Land. But God's essential identity and character restrained that anger "for the sake of my name" (this point about God's "name" is made in 20:9, 14, 22, 39, and 44).

20:18–26. Israel could not break the old pattern of unfaithfulness and idolatry. Despite God's track record of powerful intervention and care for them, the people rebelled against God's ways, which are the true way to life and blessing. God considered scattering them across the earth (20:23; recall Genesis 11:8) to control their sinful influence—certainly not bring them as a concentrated population into the Land of Promise.

The people became so evil that even the statutes God gave them were turned into damaging things (Ezek. 20:25). Over time, truth became legalistic tradition that took on a religiously distorted and spiritually destructive life of its own (think of the distorted religion of the scribes and Pharisees versus the faith of Jesus). Paul wrote about this same kind of well-meaning interpretation of truth that can morph quickly into terrible distortions of truth (Romans 1:23–25).

Rebels in the Promised Land (20:27–32)

20:27–30. Even after Israel, by God's grace, reached the land of Canaan and took possession of it, the people pursued new versions of idolatry they encountered there. Canaanite Baalism was a pagan religion and fertility cult of the worst kind (see the Book of Hosea).

20:31–32. The prophet Ezekiel heard the people of his day asking whether the gods of the Babylonians now should be followed (Ezek. 20:32a). After all, the Babylonians were winning and their gods must be the truly powerful deities in the world, right? *No*, Ezekiel said, *and if you think that way you can't hear God's word for you.* Even after all that had gone before in their history to teach them the folly of idolatry, Judah in exile was tempted to "worship wood and stone" like their Babylonian neighbors, their captors. Ezekiel himself was witnessing another sad chapter in a long saga of rebellion against God's ways.

God's Action to Intervene and Save the Rebels (20:33–44)

But God was not finished with Judah just yet. Despite their shameful historical record of spiritual shortcomings, these people were still the covenant people of God. They would once more be the recipients of God's grace. God would give them another chance.

20:33–39. These verses tell of *a new experience of "wilderness."* Just as God had brought their ancestors into the Promised Land and made them a nation, so now God once again would gather the scattered exiles from their widespread locations. Acting like a king (20:33), God would reconstitute the nation to live under God's rule. Acting like a shepherd (20:37), God would sift the flock and determine who belonged in the group of faithful ones and who was faithless and would be left outside the fold. Coming out of their wilderness, the faithful would live in the security and blessings of their king-shepherd.

20:40–44. These verses tell of *a new experience of Exodus.* As God had led Israel from Egypt to Canaan, God would lead the people out of exile and into their homeland once again. And in a restored temple in Jerusalem, God would receive the proper worship "on my holy mountain" (20:40). Note this important statement in 20:44—"you shall know that I am the LORD"—and how "I am the LORD" appears throughout the chapter (20:5, 7, 19, 20, 26, 38, 42, 44). Who God is would finally be the revelation on which the people's lives would be centered.

The pagan nations would witness this new, right relationship of God with God's people. Both the worship and the witness would be pure. The past would not be forgotten completely but would become a source of humility. Yet the relationship would be governed by God's own character of grace, not by the people's tendency toward sin. Amazing grace!

Focusing on the Meaning

It's very easy for us to sit in judgment over ancient Judah for her obvious spiritual failings. But let's look at ourselves in the mirror and ask some hard spiritual questions, questions Ezekiel might ask if he were with us today. Before we rush in to remove Judah's speck, let's examine the log in our own eye. At what points in our relationship to God are we likely to fall short, too, just as Judah did?

How easy is it for us to take for granted the rich blessings of God in our time? How do we ourselves turn our backs on God and take God's blessings with callous ingratitude or even arrogant presumptuousness? Do we believe God owes us these blessings because we are God's saved people? What are we doing to maintain the two-way relationship of mutual faithfulness we have begun with God in Christ?

Jesus died for us on the cross, yes, as God's free gift of grace. But Jesus also calls us to "take up" our own "cross daily and follow" him (Luke 9:23) so that the world might see Jesus in us. How are we doing? Are we *taking* the free gift of Jesus and also *giving* our own sacrifice as Jesus did? Or are we failing to live up to the instructions of Jesus in the New Covenant that we can understand so clearly? Love the unlovely. Respond in kindness, not in kind. Enjoy the blessings of giving that far outstrip the fun of receiving. Let go of worry and live in trust. These instructions from Jesus are so easy to understand but so difficult to follow some days.

Maybe we are not as different from Judah as we would like to think we are. A generous helping of gratitude (for Jesus' sacrifice) and a healthy dose of humility (about our ability to follow faithfully Jesus' self-giving example) would help us to learn from Judah's historical mistakes— which God told Ezekiel to review for them. Like Judah, we get a second chance, too. God is not finished with us.

TEACHING PLANS

Teaching Plan—Varied Learning Activities

Connect with Life

1. Prepare ahead of time and distribute survey sheets with these instructions at the top: *If gratitude were the only stipulation, indicate which of the following gifts you would accept.*

   Include an "accept" or "reject" box beside each line, and list items such as these: a new house; a new car; a $100,000 contribution to your retirement fund; a year's free lawn care; an "as much as you can carry" grocery shopping spree; free plane tickets to a destination of your choice; a part-time maid for five years or full-time for three; a private chef available at no cost for dinner parties; a new wardrobe, etc. (A copy of this activity is available in "Teaching Resource Items" for this study at www.baptistwaypress.org.)

After assuring class members that there are no limits on how many items they may choose, have them check the "accept" or "reject" box beside each listed item and discuss their choices with partners or small groups.

2. Ask whether anyone rejected some of the gifts on the list. If so, have them explain their reasons. Discuss why some people have trouble accepting good gifts. Transition into Bible study by asking, *What gifts did God offer the Israelites when God brought them out of Egyptian slavery? Why do you think God's people had such trouble accepting God's gifts?*

Guide Bible Study

3. Have someone read Ezekiel 20:1–3. Lead the group to consider why God refused to hear the delegation's request. Ask, *What might have helped the Israelites receive the right to inquire of the Lord?*

4. Instruct participants to make four columns on the back of the survey sheets they just used. Have participants in groups of two or three search Ezekiel 20:4–7 to find gifts of grace God had given his people. Instruct the groups to list these in a column on the back of the survey sheets and to discuss the impact the gifts should have had on the Israelites.

5. Instruct the groups to list in a parallel column examples found in Ezekiel 20:8–20 of ways the Israelites rejected God's gifts. Ask, *How might the nation's history have been different if they had valued God's grace more?* Discuss how the law itself was a gift of grace from God. Have groups describe God's response to the people's rejection. Direct groups to read and discuss question 2 in the *Study Guide*, "Why do you think the people rejected God's blessings in favor of the sinful influences of surrounding cultures?"

6. Have groups read Ezekiel 20:21–32. Discuss possible influences that prompted the Israelites to turn away from God. Have groups

refer to the small article, "Canaanite gods," and discuss reasons the Canaanite cults exerted such a pull on the Israelites. Note that immersion in the polytheistic Egyptian culture might have influenced their willingness to accept the existence of multiple gods. It is possible that they didn't see the conflict in worshiping other deities as long as they performed the rituals God wanted. Explain that to a large extent, they believed it was the rites and ceremonies that kept God happy. As long as they gave God what they thought God wanted—worship rites and ceremonies—why would God care what they did with other gods? Ask how God worked in the nation to change this perception.

Encourage Application

7. In the third and fourth columns on the backs of the survey sheets, have groups list gifts of grace God gives us today and ways modern believers reject his grace (for example, God shares his holiness with us, but we defile ourselves with worldly influences). Lead the class to identify some of the worldly influences that exert a pull on us. Then invite comments on why these influences are so attractive. Ask, *How can we resist the influences that tempt us to turn our backs on God?*

8. Have groups read and discuss questions 3–5 in the *Study Guide*. Ask individuals, if they are willing, to share their testimonies of rejecting or appreciating God's gifts of grace. Ask what they learned from their experiences that affects their spiritual growth and relationship with God.

9. Close the session by having groups pray together for God's help in recognizing, acknowledging, and appreciating the grace God continues to lavish on God's people.

Teaching Plan—Lecture and Questions

Connect with Life

1. Have members brainstorm ways people show *grace* to one another (for example, a teacher allows an overwhelmed student two or three more days to finish a school project, or a store manager cancels a finance charge for a late payment).

2. When all have shared their ideas, ask how many of those people who received grace would be inclined to reject it. Transition into Bible study by explaining that the Israelites who came out of Egypt, and their descendants, rejected every act of grace that God offered them.

Guide Bible Study

3. Have members consider this scenario: Two armies are engaged in battle. One side decides the time has come to stop fighting. It sends a delegation carrying a white flag to the other side to discuss terms for a cease fire.

4. Lead members to speculate on possible outcomes for the scenario (for example, will the opposing general receive the delegation and hear their terms, or might the general have them shot as soon as they're within rifle range, etc.).

5. Read Ezekiel 20:1–3. Lead members to describe the outcome for the delegation in this passage. Ask, *Why was God not willing to hear their inquiries? How were their motives wrong?*

6. Enlist a volunteer to read Ezekiel 20:4–7. Have members identify gifts God gave to Israel in this passage, and solicit thoughts on how God's actions demonstrated grace. Explain these verses using information in the *Study Guide* and "Bible Comments" in this *Teaching Guide.*

7. Have the class consider the case of some older schoolgirls who envied and admired the beautiful hair of a popular model. But what they didn't realize was that the model usually wore wigs or

hair extensions. No one outside of her close circle of family and hairdressers even knew what her natural hair looked like. The girls' admiration and desire to emulate her was based on lies.

Read Ezekiel 20:8–20. Discuss the lies that led the Israelites astray. Ask, *How could they have learned to differentiate God's truth from the false claims of pagan cults? What role did God intend for his law to play in keeping his people on the right track?* Explain these verses using information in the *Study Guide* and "Bible Comments" in this *Teaching Guide*.

8. Have someone read Ezekiel 20:21–32. Explain these verses using information in the *Study Guide* and "Bible Comments" in this *Teaching Guide*. Ask whether God's punishment negated his grace. Enlist volunteers to read Proverbs 3:11–12 and Hebrews 12:7–8. Discuss how divine discipline is consistent with God's grace. Then discuss how punishment is different from revenge. Ask, *What was God's motive for punishing Israel? How could God's punishment free his children from the deadly peril of sinful entrapment?*

Encourage Application

9. Lead members to reflect on their experiences with God's grace. Have individuals consider honestly how they respond to God's gifts. *Do they consistently acknowledge them and live out their gratitude daily, or do they ignore or take them for granted?* Ask members to consider this question: *How do I reject God's grace in my life, and how can I change?*

10. Allow time for members to spend several minutes in silent reflection before closing the session with prayer.

NOTES ──

1. Unless otherwise indicated, all Scripture quotations in lessons 5-8 and 11-13 are from the New Revised Standard Version.

FOCAL TEXT
Ezekiel 37:1–14

BACKGROUND
Ezekiel 37:1–14

MAIN IDEA

Ezekiel's vision of flesh coming on dry bones and the breath of life entering the dead portrayed Israel's coming restoration and revival.

QUESTION TO EXPLORE

When things seem so bad, how can we believe a better day is coming?

TEACHING AIM

To lead adults to state the meaning of Ezekiel's vision of the dry bones and to identify how it speaks to their lives

LESSON TWELVE

There's a Better Day Coming

BIBLE COMMENTS

Understanding the Context

Perhaps the most famous passage in the Book of Ezekiel, the *valley of dry bones* vision in chapter 37 has inspired artists and musicians across the 2,500 years since Ezekiel delivered that prophetic message. But what was Ezekiel saying to the people of his day? What was the historical and spiritual context for such a dramatically visual sermon?

This vision is not assigned a specific date in the book. But it opens with a scene of total devastation, a situation that struck Judah after the fall of Jerusalem in 587 B.C. The Babylonian armies utterly defeated the country, destroyed its capital city, and burned the beloved temple where Ezekiel had served as priest. He must have been devastated by the news he received among the exiles in far-off Babylon about six months later from a survivor's eyewitness report, probably in 586 B.C. (according to Ezekiel 33:21, a notation that seems to date this entire section of hope in the Book of Ezekiel).

King Nebuchadrezzar and his Babylonian armies had invaded Judah in 597 B.C. and carried off to Babylon the leaders of society, including the priest Ezekiel. That was the first deportation of exiles from Judah. The Babylonians had put into power a puppet king, Zedekiah, whom they expected to control.

When more rebellion broke out in Judah a decade later, the final and crushing devastation came down without mercy. It was a scene of death and defeat. So God called Ezekiel to voice a vision for the future that would arise out of the bones of death.

Interpreting the Scriptures

A Scene of Complete Devastation (37:1–3)

37:1–2. God led the prophet out to "the valley." We can't be certain, but perhaps it was the very same one in Babylon where Ezekiel had received God's call to be a prophet ("valley," Ezek. 37:1; or "plain," 3:22–23—the same Hebrew word). In lesson nine we read how Ezekiel encountered God's glory and received God's Spirit (3:22–24) after he had heard God's call in 593 B.C. through the throne-chariot vision of God's greatness (1:4–28). But as Ezekiel looked out over the valley that day in 586 B.C., Ezekiel found a very different scene. God's greatness on a wheeled throne in the thunderclouds was not the focus that day. No, by this time the ground of that parched valley was littered with the dried, sun-baked skeletons of God's people. Judah was defeated, exiled, dead, and not even given a decent burial.

37:3. So God posed a hypothetical question to his prophet. *Son of man* (that is, mortal human being), *do you believe these bones can ever come back to life?* The vision in front of Ezekiel was stark, and he was keenly conscious of the physical limits of human life as visible in the bones before him. So Ezekiel took the middle road with his answer. He didn't say *yes*, and he didn't say *no*. He was honest. It could go either way.

With all of the devastation and death Ezekiel had known at the hands of the Babylonian forces of destruction, these bones certainly appeared to have reached their final resting place. In human terms, the Babylonians had won, and Judah was as dead as a doornail. As a *son of man*, Ezekiel saw widespread death from the past—and not much future.

But as a prophet of God, Ezekiel could not say *no* either. After all that had happened to Judah, anything might be possible with God. So the faithful prophet responded to God by saying, *Oh God, you know where this could end up. I myself don't really know for sure. But you know.*

Prospects for a Future Beyond What Is Seen (37:4–6)

37:4–6. With that cautiously faithful openness on the part of the prophet, God instructed Ezekiel to join his voice with the power of God and to become a part of the new future. In these three verses, God previewed for Ezekiel what was about to unfold in the following events. God was going to use his prophetic spokesperson to breathe life back into what was once so dead. God's work in God's people was not finished. Death was not going to be the final word in that valley that day.

We walk by faith and not by sight is a powerful truth of Christian faith. The Old Testament faithful knew the same principle of walking with God. Ezekiel was living out his faith in God in this particular vision. All he could *see* were bones; but God *said* the people would live again. So Ezekiel preached to those skeletons as if they were the living people of God.

God was about to prove once again that "I am the LORD." Nothing could explain this event of restoration and renewal except that it was a *God thing.*

Getting the Pieces Back Together and Alive Again (37:7–10)

37:7–8. So Ezekiel started preaching to that bone yard. Then God started doing things to turn it into a different place. The "word of the LORD" (37:4) made things happen. The words of the prophet were the means. Bones began to connect to bones, in the right order. Pieces once separated were now joined together once again.

Those bones-turned-back-into-skeletons were covered with muscular flesh and then with the covering of skin on the outside. The bodies were coming together once again. The scene had changed from a valley of bones to a group of bodies.

But what good was a large collection of dead bodies? Yes, they were no longer just scattered piles of bare bones. The ligaments and muscles were in place, and the bodies were complete. But these corpses still lacked the essential ingredient of life. The structures were there, but the life itself was missing. It wasn't a bone yard anymore, but it was still a cemetery.

37:9–10. The missing secret of life was the "breath" of life (recall Genesis 2:7). The Hebrew word used here is *ruach,* and it can be used in different Old Testament contexts to mean either *spirit, breath,* or *wind.* It was a very rich term—whether applied to God, humankind, or nature. It might refer to the Spirit of God. Or to the breath of life that made humans come alive. Or to the God-created breeze that drove a sailboat across the sea or brought a cloud with its life-giving rain. It is a frequent word in the Book of Ezekiel because the prophet's ministry and the life of Judah were guided by the *ruach* of God (see Ezek. 37:1).

Once the *ruach* entered the bodies in the valley, by the powerful word and work of the Lord those re-assembled bodies stood to their feet. A new assembly of God's people had just been formed.

The Restored Hope for a Significant Future (37:11–14)

37:11. Ezekiel reported that God made the point of the vision explicitly clear: *These bones were the entire nation of Judah, thoroughly defeated and devastated.* Judah was hopeless. She seemed to be without any future prospects whatsoever.

37:12–13. But God was not finished with Judah. From their "graves" in far-away precincts like Babylon, God would call them forth to return to their homeland and rebuild their lives there. It would indeed be a *God thing*, and they would understand very clearly that "I am the LORD," God said. Only the *ruach* of God is capable of bringing life from death, victory from defeat, hope from disaster.

37:14. God's Spirit would occupy God's people when they returned home. They would live in faithfulness to God because they knew God had acted on their behalf.

This vision was realized in 538 B.C. when the Persians defeated the Babylonian Empire and allowed the exiles held in Babylon to go back home. God used Cyrus the Great—the pagan king of Persia (Isaiah 45:1–4) who issued the important Edict of Cyrus (see a summary in Ezra 1:1–4)—to bring about the restoration of Judah. The second temple was completed in 515 B.C. God was not finished with Judah.

Focusing on the Meaning

Have you ever felt you had reached a complete dead end, spiritually speaking? Perhaps the losses had mounted up and were getting much too heavy to bear. The defeats were piling up, one on top of the other, with no end in sight. The discouragement had become contagious. Warm faithfulness looked like a naïve response to the hard, cold facts. The keen disappointments in multiple people you had trusted could not even be counted since there was such a long list of them. The life of the church itself seemed to have become empty, lifeless, hopeless—it now appeared to be just a shadow of the vibrant witness it once had been in the community. The tangled bones of spiritual defeat had been baked dry in the heat of anger and alienation. If you have ever been that low in your walk of Christian discipleship, then this vision is for you.

Ezekiel surveyed the situation of Judah in Babylonian exile and looked upon a scene of almost total devastation. He had little hope. Nobody in his right mind would hold out much hope that the broken pieces of Judah could ever be restored. This former-priest-now-turned-prophet had seen every key aspect of his religious life either disappointed, displaced, or destroyed. In effect, he was looking at Judah's version of Humpty-Dumpty. No imaginable set of possible circumstances ever could put Judah together again. But the power of God's grace was not finished with Judah. Ezekiel held to a visionary calling that it would happen.

How was God's grace made known to you in your lowest times? If you *stayed a Christian* or *came back to church*—despite your period of deep spiritual devastation—then you found God's grace *somewhere*. Was it a movement of the Spirit of God that let you see that another breath of grace was still possible? Did you feel the Wind of grace in the presence of a Christian friend? Did God lead you back into Scripture and show you the fresh blowing breeze of God's truth? Was the strong sinew and muscle of a church mission trip the means for you to see God's action *stand up* in the world again? Was yours a faithful vision that refused to give up on God because God had promised never to give up on you?

Clarence Jordan (1912–1969)[1] of Koinonia Farms[2] in Americus, Georgia, stubbornly refused to quit even when the shotguns and dynamite of the Ku Klux Klan threatened the spiritual community he had invested his life to build. Despite a mounting pile of worldly evidence to the contrary—and despite the devastating power of the Babylonian armies of racism all around him—Clarence still could see, beyond the dynamite smoke, a vision of life and not death. The threat of the grave never robbed him of the promise of the resurrection.

Faith can see such visions—visions of a God whose work through God's people, however devastated they may become, is not yet finished. It's truly a *God thing*.

TEACHING PLANS

Teaching Plan—Varied Learning Activities

Connect with Life

1. Before the session, create comment cards or papers cut from a simple bone outline. To begin the session, divide the class into pairs or small groups, and distribute several bones to each group. Have them discuss factors that can lead to spiritual death or hopelessness and record them using a single word on each bone. (For example, *disappointment, anger, fear, doubt,* or *apathy.*)

2. As each group shares the words on their bones, display them in a prominent place (such as taping them to a wall or poster). Discuss how each of the terms listed can have a negative effect on Christian faith or growth. Ask what steps believers can take to prevent the *bones* from killing their relationship with God. Transition into Bible study by explaining that we can learn from the case study of Israel's fall and restoration.

Guide Bible Study

3. Ask how people tend to respond when asked a truly outlandish question to which there is no clear answer. Common reactions might vary from laughter to irritation. Enlist a volunteer to read Ezekiel 37:1–3. Ask, *How might you have reacted to God's seemingly outlandish question?* Discuss Ezekiel's response. Note that his reply reflected no amusement, suspicion, astonishment, or annoyance. He merely looked to the God who has all the answers.

4. Have the groups in step 1 read Ezekiel 37:4–6 and discuss why God involved Ezekiel in the restoration process. Groups should answer these questions: *Why didn't God just show Ezekiel the bones, pull them together, and give him the message they represented? What did it accomplish to have Ezekiel involved in the process by preaching to the bones? How might the experience have affected Ezekiel's faith or*

relationship with God? (A copy of the group assignments for steps 4 and 5 is available in "Teaching Resource Items" for this study at www.baptistwaypress.org.)

5. Direct groups to continue reading Ezekiel 37:7–10. Groups should answer these questions: *What was the role of the Spirit (ruach) in these verses? Since the word for Spirit (ruach) can be translated as breath, wind, or life, what is the symbolic significance of each portrayal? Why was the Spirit so prominent in this part of the scene? What was the Spirit's role in the life-giving process? What parallel do you see in this section to the account of humankind's creation in Genesis 2:7?*

6. Have everyone read Ezekiel 37:11–14. Then refer to and ask question 1 in the *Study Guide*, "In what ways had the people of Israel become dead and dried up like the bones in Ezekiel's vision?" Discuss factors that led to this situation. Refer back to the *bones* from the introductory activity in step 1, and ask whether any of the terms might have been applicable to Israel's situation. Have members suggest other words from Israel's experience that could be added to the bones on the wall.

7. Ask, *What would Israel's restoration look like on a practical level? How would the people act? How could the nation guard against reverting back to dry bones again?*

Encourage Application

8. Instruct groups to look at question 2 in the *Study Guide* and share their thoughts in response. Have them follow with question 3. Encourage individuals who are willing to share their experiences of God using unexpected means to help or confront them with his message.

9. Have groups discuss question 4 in the *Study Guide*, once more referring to the displayed *bones* from step 1.

10. Direct groups to continue discussion with questions 5 and 6 in the *Study Guide*. Encourage individuals to share their experiences of spiritual renewal or restoration. Close the session by having groups

pray together, especially asking God to keep their faith alive and healthy.

Teaching Plan—Lecture and Questions

Connect with Life

1. If possible, locate a recording of the spiritual known as "Dem Bones" or "Dry Bones," and begin the session by playing it for the class (if a recording is unavailable, find and make copies of the words and distribute them; websites with song lyrics are available through internet search engines if needed). Ask how many have heard the song before. Note that it has in many ways rendered this lesson's focal passage unforgettable in folk history. Ask, *Why do you think the spiritual has been so popular?* Lead the group to discuss the song's message.

2. Transition into Bible study by commenting that while the song may have trivialized Ezekiel's vision in some ways, there was nothing trivial about his experience or the powerful message God was sending through it.

Guide Bible Study

3. While a volunteer reads Ezekiel 37:1–3 aloud, have members listen for details that create the setting for the vision. Ask, *Why was it important for the description to establish that the bones were completely dead and dried up, with no hint of life?* Add insights from the *Study Guide* and "Bible Comments" in this *Teaching Guide*.

4. Read Ezekiel 37:4–6. Note that the restoration process was not merely a matter of animating dead bones, like we might see in an old low-budget horror movie. The statement "you shall know that I am the LORD" (Ezek. 37:6) implies that these re-created people would be conscious human beings, capable of thought, reason, and emotional response. Ask, *Why is that fact significant in this vision?*

Add insights on these verses from the *Study Guide* and "Bible Comments" in this *Teaching Guide.*

5. Invite someone to read Ezekiel 37:7–10. Ask, *Why do you think the process of re-creation was accomplished in two separate steps—the revival of the bones and the filling with the breath of life?* (See Gen. 2:7.) Discuss the symbolism of the breath and wind. Compare the life-giving breath in this scene with the empowering of the Spirit at the time of Ezekiel's call to prophetic ministry (Ezek. 2:2; 3:12). Discuss the role of the Spirit in giving and sustaining both physical and spiritual life. Add insights on these verses from the *Study Guide* and "Bible Comments" in this *Teaching Guide.*

6. Enlist a volunteer to read Ezekiel 37:11. Ask the class to explain the meaning of the statement, "Our bones are dried up and our hope is gone; we are cut off" (NIV84). Ask, *In what ways were Israel's "bones" dried up? Why was their hope gone? From what were they cut off?*

7. Read Ezekiel 37:12–14. Point out the parallel between verse 14 and verse 6 ("you will know that I am the LORD"). Explain that one of the reasons Israel had been cut off from God's presence was that the people had forgotten God truly was "the LORD" (literal, *Yahweh*). The worship and obedience that should have been reserved for the one true, living God, they had squandered away on worthless idols. The nation's re-creation would prove to them that God alone could give and sustain life.

Encourage Application

8. Have members think of ways the Spirit give us life today. Ask, *How does the Spirit convict us of the truth and help us remember that God is "the* LORD*"?*

9. Lead the class to suggest ways Christians can become like *dry bones.* Ask, *How do some people lose hope? What steps can we take to prevent that from happening in our spiritual lives?*

10. Allow time for members to reflect on the health of their spiritual lives before closing in prayer.

NOTES

1. See http://www.georgiaencyclopedia.org/articles/arts-culture/clarence-jordan-1912-1969. Accessed 10/3/2013. Or Google "Clarence Jordan."

2. Now Koinonia Partners. See http://koinoniapartners.org/. Accessed 10/3/2013.

FOCAL TEXT
Ezekiel 10:18–19; 11:22–23; 40:1–2; 43:1–9

BACKGROUND
Ezekiel 10:1–22; 11:22–23; 40—43

MAIN IDEA
In Ezekiel's vision, the glory of the Lord, who had departed the temple earlier, would return, signifying the restoration of Israel to live in God's presence faithfully again.

QUESTION TO EXPLORE
What would be required for us to sense that we are living in God's presence?

TEACHING AIM
To lead adults to explain the meaning of the departure and return of the glory of the Lord and to state what they need to do to live in God's presence

LESSON THIRTEEN
Living in God's Presence Again

BIBLE COMMENTS

Understanding the Context

At the very center of Ezekiel's religious understanding was the fact that God's *name* (that is, God's identity and character) had been revealed clearly to God's people throughout their history with God. Equally important was the understanding that God occupied a place of Presence in the midst of God's people—in the inner sanctum of the temple, the holy of holies. Ezekiel's theology of God, fashioned when he was a priest, clearly carried over into his theology as a prophet.

Ezekiel's venue had changed—from the temple courts in Jerusalem to the Jewish precinct in far-away Babylon. His role assignment had changed—from a priest who offered sacrifices in normal times to a prophet who pronounced sermons in the most difficult days. But his essential theology of God and God's people did not change.

What was the core of Ezekiel's beliefs that remained constant across his entire lifetime of ministry and witness? This lesson gives us a window into the prophet's spiritual heart as he emphasized the vital presence (or absence) of God with God's people.

The God of the Exodus and Sinai had given his people Israel clear instructions for their covenant relationships to God and to one another. But in lesson eleven on Ezekiel 20 we studied Ezekiel's recital of the long history of failure among God's people to keep that covenant faithfully and consistently.

In Ezekiel 8—11 we read a shocking account of the covenant dis-obedience and horribly blatant idolatry being practiced in Judah—and in the temple in Jerusalem itself—during Ezekiel's time (probably 591 B.C. if we apply the date in Ezekiel 8:1). Because the sin was so blatant, God would not stay near it. Thus God soon departed from the temple where he was supposed to dwell in the midst of God's covenant people. We find two references to the moment that God left the temple behind and the glory of the Lord departed from God's people (Ezek. 10:18–19 and 11:22–23).

Interpreting the Scriptures

The Holy God Leaves the Filthy Temple (10:18–19; 11:22–23)

Ezekiel was physically located in Babylon and lived among the exiles there. But the Spirit of God transported him in an ecstatic vision, lifting him up and carrying him to Jerusalem so that he could observe the temple and all of the misbehavior that was occurring there. Ezekiel 8:1–4 tells of Ezekiel's arrival in Jerusalem by the Spirit, and Ezekiel 11:24–25 of his return to Babylon by the Spirit.

In one of the most dramatic and chilling statements in all of the Bible, God left the holy of holies where God had lived inside, first in the mobile tabernacle (the tent of meeting) and later in the permanent temple. This was the sacred spot—in the very presence of God—where the priest offered the blood offering each year on the Day of Atonement, covering the sins of the people (Leviticus 16) before the eyes of Holy God.

As the culmination of Ezekiel's visionary visit to Jerusalem and its temple courts, Ezekiel watched as God actually left the temple inner sanctum and moved out through the "east gate" (Ezek. 10:19) to hover over the Mount of Olives just east of the city. As long as the terrible and idolatrous behavior took place in the temple, God would remove himself from any proximity to it.

When God had finished showing Ezekiel the corrupt state of temple practices in Jerusalem, the Spirit (*ruach*) transported him in his vision back to Babylon (Chaldea) and his fellow exiles there. Then he reported to them what he had seen in his visionary journey to visit God's house (11:24–25).

The Temple Is Restored for the Future (Ezekiel 40:1–2)

In Ezekiel 40—48 we read finely detailed descriptions of the prophet's idealized vision for the future of the entire land of Judah—but especially Jerusalem and the temple precincts. Ezekiel foresaw a wonderfully restored land after God's grace-filled intervention had reversed the devastation of defeat and had removed the distance of the Exile. As a priest, Ezekiel was particularly concerned in his vision with a restored temple where Holy God would dwell once again amidst his holy covenant people.

The date given for the vision of the restored temple was 572 B.C. (40:1–2). Ezekiel once again was transported in a vision to Jerusalem, just as before when he had observed the sin that was rampant there (Ezek. 8—11). But now, almost two decades later, he saw a new city and a pure temple. The former priest, who knew every square foot of Solomon's temple, where he had once served, described in exquisite detail a beautifully restored future temple.

On arrival in Jerusalem, Ezekiel was met by a heavenly messenger who served as his guide through the temple area. This guide told him to remember and report all he saw to God's people.

Ezekiel 40—48 represents the biblical account of what Ezekiel saw in his vision of a restored land, purified from the sins of previous generations. With its restored temple at the center of the holy city, it was a beautiful and perfect vision of the ideal future.

In Ezekiel 40:5—42:20, the gates and courtyards of the temple are described with their specific measurements. Ezekiel envisioned a day in the future when every aspect of temple worship would be just right. Particular architectural details are mentioned. For example, the prescribed sacrifices would be prepared and offered on special tables (40:38–43). The layout of the temple itself, complete with its various dimensions, is given (41:1–26). Even the living quarters of the priests are located in the floor plan, too (40:44–49; 42:1–20).

The Return of the Presence of the Lord (43:1–11)

But what use could be served by such a perfectly planned temple if God were not present within it? For ancient Israel, the powerful presence of Holy God was their salvation. So the return of God to dwell in the newly restored temple was vitally important.

43:1–5. Ezekiel's heavenly guide for his vision led him to the east gate— the same portal from which God had departed from the former, corrupt temple in Ezekiel's earlier vision of the sin being committed there (10:18–19). So Ezekiel was in place to witness the very moment when the Lord returned to the temple through that same east gate. Falling on his face before Holy God, the prophet saw enough to describe the sights and sounds of the arrival of God's glorious presence.

43:6–9. Then Ezekiel heard God speak! God told the prophet that this temple would be God's dwelling place forever among God's people. Too, the people of God would not sin and defile the place of God's presence ever again. God strongly challenged the people to end their sinfulness and to continue forever to dwell in God's presence.

The careful design and detailed perfection of the temple would function in this ideal future to remind the people of God to leave their sin behind (43:10–11). They would participate in faithful obedience to God and thus enjoy eternity in God's house. As a restored and purified people, Israel should never be separated again from the presence of God.

Focusing on the Meaning

Have you, or the church you were involved in, ever been through a period in your spiritual journey when it seemed *the glory had departed*? God seemed to be withdrawn and so far away. The human failure and sins against God's ideals appeared to have spelled doom on any healthy spiritual life for everyone involved. The wrongdoing by corrupt person(s) or bad decisions was so complete and devastating that it seemed not even God would bother to stay around to see how it all might come out.

In Ezekiel's thought, the presence and revelation of God's holy and righteous self was absolutely vital to God's people and their future. In God's instructions to the people of Israel, God had told them clearly, "You shall be holy, for I the LORD your God am holy" (Lev. 19:2). The people of God were to reflect the presence of God in their witness of words and actions. God would stay near them as long as they were reflecting in their lives the Presence of God.

If Judah were going to follow God and truly be God's people, then God must remain nearby—God must be there with them along the journey. Also, just as important, Judah must remain faithful and close to God. Trying to go it alone without God is a disastrous, self-defeating approach to the spiritual life.

Two of the first followers of Jesus learned the power of God's presence at a low moment when they thought the glory had departed. Thinking that Jesus was dead and buried, they discovered just how life-changing the presence of the Risen Christ would be. Luke 24:13–35 tells about their discouragement over the departure of the presence of Jesus from their lives.

But Jesus was alive again. Jesus came alongside them on their journey and walked with them. He entered into their conversation and was listening, leading, and teaching them during their pilgrimage.

The resurrected Lord is not confined to an inner sanctum of a holy building in a sacred city. Jesus is alive and walks with us every step of every day as we allow him as Holy Spirit to be our Companion and Guide. And just like those two followers of Jesus on that first Easter afternoon, because of the presence of Christ we can experience a walk that is rejuvenated and a witness that is enthusiastic and effective.

TEACHING PLANS

Teaching Plan—Varied Learning Activities

Connect with Life

1. Refer to and tell the story about the restored chapel in the introduction to the lesson in the *Study Guide*. Transition into Bible study by reading the last paragraph in the story plus the *Study Guide's* Main Idea.

Guide Bible Study

2. Enlist someone to read Ezekiel 10:18–19. Ask members to describe what was happening and why. Recall that the cherubim were guardians of God's throne. When God's glory departed from the temple, they were no longer needed there.

3. Have members read Ezekiel 11:22–23. Ask, *What was taking place in that scene?* (The glory of God abandoned the temple and the

city of Jerusalem. The mountain east of the city was the Mount of Olives, which would figure prominently in the passion of Jesus. Use a map to locate the temple and the Mount of Olives. Explain Ezekiel 10:18–19 and 11:22–23 further by using information in the *Study Guide* and "Bible Comments" in this *Teaching Guide*.

4. Ask: *Why did God withdraw from the temple, which was known as the house of God?* Divide the class into groups and have them identify from Ezekiel 8 offenses committed against the temple. Lead the class to note especially the following passages: Ezekiel 8:5 (probably the statue of Asherah that Josiah removed, 2 Kings 23:6); Ezekiel 8:9–12 (Egyptian worship of reptiles and animals); Ezekiel 8:14 (worship of the Sumerian god Tammuz); Ezekiel 8:16 (sun worship). As groups report, record the findings on a board. Referring to the list, have each group prepare and share a one-line summary of the unrighteousness that compelled God to withdraw his glory from the temple.

5. Enlist a volunteer to read Ezekiel 40:1–2. Point out that the passage refers to Mount Zion, the sacred area that was the site of the temple. Explain that the city-like structure Ezekiel saw (Ezek. 40:2) was probably an idealized, restored vision of Solomon's temple. Ask: *Why do you think God gave Ezekiel a vision of Jerusalem and its temple, since they both had already been destroyed and the people were exiles in Babylon?*

6. Invite someone to read Ezekiel 43:1–5 and someone else to read Ezekiel 43:6–9. Assign half the class to listen for what Ezekiel saw and half the class to listen for what Ezekiel heard. Receive reports first on what Ezekiel saw and then on what Ezekiel heard. Explain the passage by using information in the *Study Guide* and "Bible Comments" in this *Teaching Guide*.

Encourage Application

7. Note that the sins Israel committed were punishable by death. Yet God's mercy tempered his anger. He withheld the full punishment Israel deserved and in love restored the broken relationship. The "glory of the LORD" had departed from the temple earlier (Ezek.

10:18–19; 11:22–23), but now Ezekiel saw the "glory of the God of Israel" (43:2) return.

8. Point out how the cross represents God's fullest expression of wrath against sin, but also shows the depth of God's love and mercy. Note that although we all deserve death as sinners, the sacrifice of Christ's blood made forgiveness possible. With relationship restored, God's glory comes to live in us. We ourselves become God's temple. Close the session in prayer

Teaching Plan—Lecture and Questions

Connect with Life

1. Share this biographical sketch:

   "Amazing Grace" is one of the most beloved hymns of all time, and yet the man who wrote it once captained a slave ship. John Newton had given up on religion. However, caught in a violent storm during a voyage, he experienced a "great deliverance." By the grace of God, not only was his ship saved, but he himself came to faith in Christ. He left the sea and eventually joined the campaign to abolish slavery.

2. Note that Newton lived out the truth expressed by Paul, "If anyone is in Christ, there is a new creation" (2 Corinthians 5:17). Point out that we have seen God's transforming power in our study of the Book of Jeremiah, especially in the promise of a "new covenant" (Jeremiah 31:31). Now, in this lesson in Ezekiel, we see God's transforming power in the departure and then the return of God's presence to the temple in Jerusalem. Transition into Bible study by explaining that at the heart of Ezekiel's prophecy was God's promise to save Israel from the wreckage of their moral and spiritual apostasy. Although God's people might give up on God, God never gives up on his people.

Guide Bible Study

3. Enlist someone to read Ezekiel 10:18–19. After the reading, point out the following:

   a. The "glory of the LORD" was not a mere attribute of God. It was God himself. (To illustrate, when people address their king as *your majesty*, the *majesty* does not refer to a characteristic of the king, but to the king himself.)

   b. It must have been devastating for Ezekiel's contemporaries to hear that God was abandoning the temple that had been his dwelling place all their lives. If they could not find God in the temple, where would they find him? With God gone, they were left without hope.

4. Have someone read Ezekiel 11:22–23. Ask, *Why did God's glory leave the city as well as the temple?* Have the class look at verse 21 for the answer. Explain that the Israelites had left God no choice but to abandon that city because they prostituted his temple. Explain 10:18–19 and 11:22–23 further by using information in the *Study Guide* and "Bible Comments" in this *Teaching Guide.*

5. Invite someone to read Ezekiel 40:1–2. In a vision, Ezekiel was transported to "a very high mountain" overlooking Jerusalem. Ask whether anyone can identify this mountain. Have everyone look at Micah 4:1, which describes Mount Zion. The "high mountain" in Ezekiel's vision was Mount Zion, site of the temple.

6. Read Ezekiel 43:1–9. Ask, *What significance is there in God's "glory" entering by the temple's east gate?* Note that in this passage the events of Ezekiel 10:18–19 and 11:22–23 are reversed. God's "glory" entered the temple from the same direction God had departed. Explain that God's return confirmed that the peoples' sins had been forgiven. God's withdrawal from the temple was not abandonment of his people but prepared the way for God to manifest his presence under new circumstances. The Presence that had forsaken the temple pursued the people into exile, once again showing divine compassion and willingness to restore them. Explain the passage further as needed by using information in the *Study Guide* and "Bible Comments" in this *Teaching Guide.*

Encourage Application

7. Read 1 Corinthians 6:19. Lead members to consider these questions: *Am I a temple where God feels honored? Are there idols in my life that take away God's glory?* Have everyone silently read question 6 in the *Study Guide*, "What does 'living in God's presence' look like on a practical level? How does the Spirit's involvement affect our attitudes and actions?" Ask the group to consider the implications for their lives. Invite comments. Refer to and read the closing paragraph under the heading, "Implications and Actions," in the *Study Guide*. Close the session in a prayer for greater sensitivity to the Lord's presence and leading.

FOCAL TEXT
Luke 24:1–10, 33–39, 44–48

BACKGROUND
Luke 24:1–52

MAIN IDEA
Jesus' resurrection shows he is truly the Christ of God, the fulfillment of God's promises in Scripture.

QUESTION TO EXPLORE
What makes Jesus' resurrection so important?

TEACHING AIM
To lead the class to tell what Jesus' resurrection shows about who Jesus is, what Jesus does, and how we are to respond

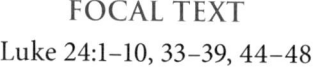

EASTER LESSON

What Jesus' Resurrection Shows Us

BIBLE COMMENTS

Understanding the Context

With horrifying speed Jesus was arrested, tried, and crucified. A week that began with a joyful royal procession into Jerusalem (Luke 19:28–44) ended with Jesus' death on a Roman cross (23:26–49). Luke records that as the Lord hung on the cross, darkness covered the land from noon to three p.m. (23:44). The darkness reflected the sin and sorrow of the day as humanity crucified the Lord's Anointed (see 22:53). It also reflected the mood of Jesus' followers, particularly the apostles. Despite Jesus' warnings to them that he would suffer and die in Jerusalem (9:22; 17:25), his execution stunned them. In Luke the final words spoken at the scene of the crucifixion are those of a pagan Roman centurion who said, "Surely this was a righteous man"(23:47).[1]

Luke tells how "a good and upright man" named Joseph of Arimathea went to Pilate to gain custody of Jesus' body (23:50). Joseph was a member of the Jewish ruling council who disagreed with their actions in relation to Jesus. After Pilate granted his request, Joseph took Jesus' body down from the cross, wrapped it in linen cloth, and placed it in a tomb cut in rock (23:50–53). The tomb had not been used before. Although Luke doesn't mention it in chapter 23, Joseph evidently rolled a large stone in front of the tomb's entrance (see 24:2). This precaution was customary because it kept animals from harming the body.

The women who had been with Jesus since he began his public ministry in Galilee followed Joseph and saw where the tomb was. They went home and began to prepare spices to place on Jesus' body but stopped working when the Sabbath began.

None of the women or the apostles went to the tomb the next day because it was a Sabbath. It was a horrible time of despair as Jesus' followers felt shock and grief. They didn't know that at dawn on the first day of the week, their darkness and sorrow would turn to light and joy.

Interpreting the Scriptures

Introduction

Nearly all of Luke's narrative of Jesus' resurrection is unique to the Gospel of Luke, with the exceptions of 24:1–6, 9–10. His account divides into three episodes: the empty tomb (24:1–12), the appearance on the road to Emmaus (24:13–35), and the appearance to all the disciples (24:36–53). Only the first of these episodes has parallels with the other Gospels, and even it is distinctive, particularly in relation to Mark.

The Empty Tomb (24:1–12)

24:1. "On the first day of the week," Sunday, "very early in the morning' (the Greek says *deep dawn*), the women went to the tomb to complete their ministry to Jesus' body.

24:2–3. The women were surprised to find that the stone that had been rolled in front of the entrance of the tomb had been rolled away. In the early morning light, they entered the tomb but didn't find Jesus' body.

24:4. For Luke, the empty tomb by itself didn't produce faith. The women wondered what had happened. The consistent theme of the resurrection accounts in all the Gospels is that none of Jesus' followers expected him to rise from the dead following his crucifixion.

Suddenly, two men in brilliant white clothes stood beside them. It was as if they burst in on them. Luke used the word "men" to describe angels when they appeared in human form (see Acts 1:10; 10:30). In Luke 24:23, Cleopas and his companion called them angels.

24:5–8. The angels mildly rebuked the women for not understanding what had happened. They should have remembered Jesus' promise to them that he would rise again. Luke records that Jesus predicted his death and his resurrection on the third day in 9:22 and 18:32–33. When the angels mentioned what Jesus said, the women "remembered his words."

24:9–10. When the women came back from the tomb, they told what they had witnessed to the Eleven and the other followers of Christ gathered with them. In all the Gospels women were the first to hear the good news of Jesus' resurrection and the first to proclaim it. Ancient people thought women were unreliable witnesses. Their testimony wasn't accepted in court. Yet God chose to honor women by placing them in this position. Luke went to special lengths to show the role women played in Jesus' ministry (see Luke 8:1–3; 21:1–4; 23:49, 55–57) despite the low esteem in which men held them.

The other Gospels give the names of the women at the beginning of their resurrection narratives. All four Gospels place Mary Magdalene first (Matthew 28:1; Mark 16:1; Luke 24:2; John 20:2). Matthew, Mark, and Luke all mention "Mary, the mother of James," or "the other Mary." Only Luke mentions Joanna (Luke also mentions her in 8:3). Only Mark mentions Salome.

24:11. The word Luke used for "nonsense" refers to *delirious talk*. It sounded like words from people who had lost their minds.

24:12. Although Peter didn't believe what the women said, he ran to the tomb to examine it himself. He saw Jesus' burial clothes lying by themselves and went away "wondering . . . what had happened."

Again, all the Gospel accounts emphasize that even Jesus' closest followers didn't expect him to rise from the dead. Why was this so? It could have been that when Jesus made these predictions they didn't understand him to be talking about a resurrection separate from the general resurrection of the dead.

Appearance on the Road to Emmaus (24:13–32)

24:13–16, This account is unique to Luke. The two on the road were disciples of Jesus. Emmaus was "about seven miles" northwest of Jerusalem. As they walked along, they talked about everything that had happened to Jesus in Jerusalem. The Lord himself came up and began to walk with him, but "they were kept from recognizing him."

24:17–24. Jesus asked them what they were talking about, and Cleopas asked how he could have been to Jerusalem and not have known the things that had happened there. Jesus asked, "What things?" They responded by giving a summary of Jesus' life, arrest, trial, and crucifixion. In verse 21 they noted that they had hoped that Jesus would be the one who would redeem Israel, but it appeared that he wasn't. But they had heard an amazing report from "some of our women."

24:25–27. Jesus responded by telling the two that they didn't believe all that the prophets had said, and therefore, they didn't understand the Messiah's mission. They thought the Messiah's mission was to free them from Rome. But the prophets said that the Messiah had to suffer the things they had described and enter the Father's glory. Jesus started with Moses, meaning the first five books of the Old Testament, and went through "all the Prophets," showing the two men how the Scriptures spoke of his suffering, death, and resurrection.

24:28–32. As the two approached the village where they were going, the stranger acted as if he were going farther. But they compelled him to stay with them. During the evening meal, Jesus took the bread and broke it. Something about the way he did that and/or the way he pronounced the blessing revealed his identity to them. Whatever had obscured their recognition of him went away. Just as they recognized him to be Jesus, he disappeared.

Appearance to the Eleven in Jerusalem (24:33–49)

24:33–35. Although the hour was late, the two followers immediately set out for Jerusalem to see the other disciples. They found the Eleven gathered together and told them what they had experienced. For the two, their experience was definitive proof that Jesus was alive.

In verse 34 they mentioned an appearance of the Lord to Simon. Luke doesn't give an account of this appearance and none of the other Gospels mention it, but the Apostle Paul referred to it in 1 Corinthians 15:5.

24:36. Suddenly, Jesus appeared in their midst. He probably spoke the traditional Jewish greeting, *Shalom*, which means "peace be with you."

24:37–39. At first the disciples were startled and frightened, thinking they had seen a disembodied spirit. Such an apparition would not have comforted them. The only thing that would have convinced them was a resurrection. Jesus first sought to convince them that it was he. Following that, Jesus sought to show them that he had a real body.

24:40–43. Jesus gave them two signs to show that he had a real body: he invited them to touch him, and he allowed them to see him eat.

24:44–49. These verses probably condense what Jesus said to the apostles between the resurrection and ascension. It's difficult to know what he said that evening and what he said at later times. He reminded them of what he had told them before his death.

24:50–53. Jesus' ascension occurred in the area of the Mount of Olives. As the Gospel of Luke ends, the disciples are in Jerusalem, joyfully worshiping in the temple. On the day of Pentecost, the Holy Spirit would empower them to fulfill the mission Christ gave them (see Acts 2).

Focusing on the Meaning

The resurrection of the Lord Jesus Christ is the most important event recorded in the Scriptures. The Apostle Paul wrote in 1 Corinthians 15:17–19 that if Christ wasn't raised, our faith is futile and we are still in our sins. Luke made several points about this critical event: Jesus' followers didn't expect it, it was predicted in the Law and the Prophets, and Jesus appeared to his followers in a resurrected body. Consider each of these points.

First, Jesus' followers didn't expect him to rise from the dead. We can judge the disciples harshly for their lack of understanding, but we need to remember that something like this had never happened. The disciples believed in a general resurrection of the dead at the end of the age, but they didn't expect their Lord to experience an individual resurrection.

Second, the Law and the Prophets predicted Jesus' death and resurrection. These events were part of God's salvation history going back to the Garden of Eden. Jesus was the fulfillment of all God's promises to

Israel. When we follow Christ, we become a part of God's work in history from the beginning.

Third, Luke makes it clear that Jesus appeared to his disciples in a resurrected body. For Jews, real life was life in a body. Jesus' return as a spirit or ghost would have been no comfort to them. Jesus wasn't a ghost. The disciples could touch him, and he ate a fish! For the Jews the resurrection of the body was part of the end of the world, and so Jesus' resurrection showed that the general resurrection of the dead at the end of the age had begun. We who have faith in the risen Christ know that we will rise in a similar fashion at the end of the age. This hope motivates us to serve Christ intensely and self-sacrificially in the present. We have faith that our lives won't end in death but will continue forever in resurrected bodies. In the meantime, we join with the angels, the women, the disciples, and the apostles in proclaiming to the world the good news, "The Lord has risen!"

TEACHING PLANS

Teaching Plan—Varied Learning Activities

Connect with Life

1. Before the day of class, scan the local news for Easter-related events in your community or city. What are other churches doing to celebrate Easter? Is there a local Easter egg hunt? Bring clippings or print out a few news stories or announcements from the internet. As your students arrive, welcome them and make sure they have printed copies of Luke 24. Tell them about some of the local observances of Easter as they gather, passing around the clippings and printouts.

2. Lead the group to discuss ways in which they celebrate Easter with their family or friends. Do they observe any special traditions? List those on a markerboard or poster as they name them. Point out that

the celebration of Easter varies widely by churches and around the world, but that no matter the manner of celebration it is the most important of all the Christian holidays because of the significance of the resurrection. Transition to Bible study by asking the group to consider, *What is the significance of the resurrection to you?*

Guide Bible Study

3. Say, *The resurrection is important. Let's take some time to read about the first Easter as Luke portrays it. In this lesson, we're going to focus on three passages from the larger story of Easter.* Display the following outline on a marker board or easel:
   - Luke 24:1–10—Roll Away Your Stone
   - Luke 24:33–39—The Big Reveal
   - Luke 24:44–48—Prophecies and Promise Fulfilled

4. Divide your class into three groups, assigning one group to each of the passages above.[2] Ask the class to take turns reading the passages or read them aloud yourself. Read all three passages at once, encouraging each group to pay particular attention to its assigned section. Once you've completed the readings, pass out three or four pieces of paper to each group, along with several markers. Give your learners the following instructions:
   - Read your assigned passage again.
   - Imagine you are directing a dramatic film on Luke 24 and will need to create storyboards of the scene to portray the action that happens. Figures can be simple stick figures, or as elaborate as you would like.
   - Choose actors and actresses whom you'd like to see portray the people in your passage.
   - Be imaginative and discuss the set, lighting, makeup, and soundtrack, as time allows.
   - Plan to present storyboards to the larger group and narrate the action when the activity is complete.

(A copy of the group instructions is available in "Teaching Resource Items" for this study at www.baptistwaypress.org.)

Allow time for groups to complete the exercise and then present their work in sequence with the passage. Encourage applause and affirm each presentation.

Encourage Application

5. Choose questions from the *Study Guide* to lead a discussion about the story the groups have presented. Familiarize yourself with the questions in advance of the lesson so you can touch on areas the presentations in step four above may have missed. Be patient as learners arrive at answers to these questions, and avoid the temptation to answer the questions yourself.

6. Close by using the small article, "Everyday Encounters," from the *Study Guide* about the "Emmaus" places where Jesus reveals himself. Ask them to think of places where they've seen Jesus revealed.

7. Close with an encouraging prayer that asks God to help each person be on the lookout for "Emmaus" revelations of Jesus in the coming week. After the prayer, ask them to come back next week and share their observations. Alternatively, if your class has a group e-mail list, suggest they share observations with one another throughout the week.

Teaching Plan—Lecture and Questions

Connect with Life

1. Before students arrive display the following outline on a marker-board, chalkboard, or poster:
   - Luke 24:1–10—Roll Away Your Stone
   - Luke 24:33–39—The Big Reveal
   - Luke 24:44–48—Prophecies and Promise Fulfilled

   As learners arrive, invite them to find the passages in their own Bible or in the *Study Guide*. Encourage them to begin reading the passages while they wait for everyone to arrive.

2. Ask: *What are some of the ways you have celebrated Easter?* Ask about family traditions, regional or national customs, and traditions particular to churches of which they may have been a part previously. Have an example of an Easter tradition familiar to you if they are slow getting started. Once you have gathered a few examples, say, *Easter is celebrated in different ways by different people. In this lesson we are studying the Easter story from Luke 24, which gives different details than the other Gospels.*

    Encourage your students to be on the lookout for two empty tomb scenes and two resurrection appearance scenes in this study.

Guide Bible Study

3. Enlist a volunteer to read Luke 24:1–10, or read it aloud yourself. Say: *This is the first empty tomb scene. Let's name who was there.* Allow students plenty of time to come up with Mary Magdalene, Joanna, Mary the mother of James, and the "others with them" found in verse 8.

    Ask: *What did the women bring with them to the tomb?* (Spices, for the burial of the body of Jesus)

    Say, *When they arrived at the tomb, the body of Jesus was missing. As they stood there perplexed, "two men" appeared in a dazzling fashion. The women bowed down with their faces to the ground.* Ask, *Why do you think the women did that?* (Probably out of reverence, indicating that these "men" were angels or messengers from God).

    Enlist a volunteer to step up to a markerboard or easel of paper. Tell the class you will read Luke 24:6 aloud. As you read, ask learners to listen for all the things the angels prompted the women to remember. The volunteer should record the items the class calls out. Read verse 6 aloud, pausing for responses.

    Ask: *What are the three things the angels reminded the women of concerning Jesus?* (That he would be handed over to sinners, would be crucified, and would rise again on the third day) Say: *As the women's memories were prompted, they were motivated to action. They'd seen the empty tomb, interacted with the angels, and remembered that Jesus had foretold all of this.*

4. Read Luke 24:11–12 aloud and say, *They returned with the news, but only Peter took action to investigate their claims for himself.* Then offer a summary of the story of the walk to Emmaus in Luke 24:13–32. Highlight the following points:
   - Cleopas and an unnamed friend were walking to Emmaus. Jesus came alongside them in their journey, but they were not able to perceive that it was Jesus.
   - They discussed the events of the recent days, including the crucifixion and rumors of the missing body of Jesus.
   - Jesus interpreted all the things that had happened, referring to the Scriptures "concerning himself" (Luke 24:27).
   - They invited Jesus to stay with them that evening on the road, and as they ate together they recognized Jesus as he broke the bread.

5. Read aloud or invite a volunteer to read Luke 24:33–39. Say: *The text tells us they wasted no time in returning to Jerusalem ("that same hour"), and arrived to find quite a stir. The disciples were making claims about Jesus being resurrected. Then Cleopas and his companion shared their news of encountering the risen Jesus.* Ask: *In this chapter in Luke, who were the people who were now making claims about the resurrection?* List them on the markerboard or poster as students name Mary Magdalene, Mary mother of James, Joanna, "other" women, eleven disciples, Simon Peter, Cleopas, and the unnamed friend of Cleopas. Prompt them as needed. Ask: *What does this growing list of eyewitnesses suggest about the resurrection of Jesus?* Allow time for discussion.

6. Summarize Luke 24:36–43 by describing Jesus' entry into the room, what he told the gathered disciples, and what he did, giving special attention to the parts of the story that point to a bodily resurrection. Ask: *Why would Jesus' allowing the disciples to touch him and Jesus' eating food be so important to Luke?* (Proves the resurrection was real, that it was a bodily resurrection, that Jesus was not an apparition of a ghost or spirit, that Jesus was alive and well)

Encourage Application

7. Read aloud or have a volunteer read Luke 24:44–48. Ask: *What did Jesus say about his purpose? What would be the consequence of his death and resurrection?* (Repentance and forgiveness of sin proclaimed to all nations) *What mission did Jesus give to the disciples?* (That they would be the ones to proclaim the message of forgiveness) *What were they to wait upon?* (The coming of the Holy Spirit, as the Father had promised)

8. Refer to question 8 in the *Study Guide*, "Is the mission that Jesus gave the disciples still a mission for disciples today? Has the mission changed? How might the mission have changed?" Lead the group to discuss these questions. Then ask, *Is the mission of spreading the message of forgiveness alive and real for us? How might we live that out on a daily basis? What is the church's role in doing this in our community?*

9. Close with a prayer that encourages the group to look for ways in which Jesus reveals himself in the coming week.

N O T E S ————————————————————————————————

1. Unless otherwise indicated, all Scripture quotations in lessons 9 and 10 and the Easter lesson are from the New International Version (1984 edition).

2. Six or fewer people in each group. Form additional groups with duplicate assignments if attendance is larger than eighteen.

How to Order More Bible Study Materials

It's easy! Just fill in the following information. For additional Bible study materials available both in print and online, see www.baptistwaypress.org, or get a complete order form of available print materials—including Spanish materials—by calling 1-866-249-1799 or e-mailing baptistway@texasbaptists.org.

Title of item	Price	Quantity	Cost
This Issue:			
Jeremiah and Ezekiel: Prophets of Judgment and Hope—Study Guide (BWP001172)	$3.95	_____	_____
Jeremiah and Ezekiel: Prophets of Judgment and Hope—Large Print Study Guide (BWP001173)	$4.25	_____	_____
Jeremiah and Ezekiel: Prophets of Judgment and Hope—Teaching Guide (BWP001174)	$4.95	_____	_____
Additional Issues Available:			
Growing Together in Christ—Study Guide (BWP001036)	$3.25	_____	_____
Growing Together in Christ—Teaching Guide (BWP001038)	$3.75	_____	_____
Guidance for the Seasons of Life—Study Guide (BWP001157)	$3.95	_____	_____
Guidance for the Seasons of Life—Large Print Study Guide (BWP001158)	$4.25	_____	_____
Guidance for the Seasons of Life—Teaching Guide (BWP001159)	$4.95	_____	_____
Living Generously for Jesus' Sake—Study Guide (BWP001137)	$3.95	_____	_____
Living Generously for Jesus' Sake—Large Print Study Guide (BWP001138)	$4.25	_____	_____
Living Generously for Jesus' Sake—Teaching Guide (BWP001139)	$4.95	_____	_____
Living Faith in Daily Life—Study Guide (BWP001095)	$3.55	_____	_____
Living Faith in Daily Life—Large Print Study Guide (BWP001096)	$3.95	_____	_____
Living Faith in Daily Life—Teaching Guide (BWP001097)	$4.25	_____	_____
Participating in God's Mission—Study Guide (BWP001077)	$3.55	_____	_____
Participating in God's Mission—Large Print Study Guide (BWP001078)	$3.95	_____	_____
Participating in God's Mission—Teaching Guide (BWP001079)	$3.95	_____	_____
Profiles in Character—Study Guide (BWP001112)	$3.55	_____	_____
Profiles in Character—Large Print Study Guide (BWP001113)	$4.25	_____	_____
Profiles in Character—Teaching Guide (BWP001114)	$4.95	_____	_____
Genesis: People Relating to God—Study Guide (BWP001088)	$2.35	_____	_____
Genesis: People Relating to God—Large Print Study Guide (BWP001089)	$2.75	_____	_____
Genesis: People Relating to God—Teaching Guide (BWP001090)	$2.95	_____	_____
Ezra, Haggai, Zechariah, Nehemiah, Malachi—Study Guide (BWP001071)	$3.25	_____	_____
Ezra, Haggai, Zechariah, Nehemiah, Malachi—Large Print Study Guide (BWP001072)	$3.55	_____	_____
Ezra, Haggai, Zechariah, Nehemiah, Malachi—Teaching Guide (BWP001073)	$3.75	_____	_____
Psalms: Songs from the Heart of Faith—Study Guide (BWP001152)	$3.95	_____	_____
Psalms: Songs from the Heart of Faith—Large Print Study Guide (BWP001153)	$4.25	_____	_____
Psalms: Songs from the Heart of Faith—Teaching Guide (BWP001154)	$4.95	_____	_____
Amos. Hosea, Isaiah, Micah: Calling for Justice, Mercy, and Faithfulness—Study Guide (BWP001132)	$3.95	_____	_____
Amos. Hosea, Isaiah, Micah: Calling for Justice, Mercy, and Faithfulness—Large Print Study Guide (BWP001133)	$4.25	_____	_____
Amos. Hosea, Isaiah, Micah: Calling for Justice, Mercy, and Faithfulness—Teaching Guide (BWP001134)	$4.95	_____	_____
The Gospel of Matthew: A Primer for Discipleship—Study Guide (BWP001127)	$3.95	_____	_____
The Gospel of Matthew: A Primer for Discipleship—Large Print Study Guide (BWP001128)	$4.25	_____	_____
The Gospel of Matthew: A Primer for Discipleship—Teaching Guide (BWP001129)	$4.95	_____	_____
The Gospel of Mark: People Responding to Jesus—Study Guide (BWP001147)	$3.95	_____	_____
The Gospel of Mark: People Responding to Jesus—Large Print Study Guide (BWP001148)	$4.25	_____	_____
The Gospel of Mark: People Responding to Jesus—Teaching Guide (BWP001149)	$4.95	_____	_____
The Gospel of Luke: Jesus' Personal Touch—Study Guide (BWP001167)	$3.95	_____	_____
The Gospel of Luke: Jesus' Personal Touch—Large Print Study Guide (BWP001168)	$4.25	_____	_____
The Gospel of Luke: Jesus' Personal Touch—Teaching Guide (BWP001169)	$4.95	_____	_____
The Gospel of John: Light Overcoming Darkness, Part One—Study Guide (BWP001104)	$3.55	_____	_____
The Gospel of John: Light Overcoming Darkness, Part One—Large Print Study Guide (BWP001105)	$3.95	_____	_____
The Gospel of John: Light Overcoming Darkness, Part One—Teaching Guide (BWP001106)	$4.50	_____	_____
The Gospel of John: Light Overcoming Darkness, Part Two—Study Guide (BWP001109)	$3.55	_____	_____
The Gospel of John: Light Overcoming Darkness, Part Two—Large Print Study Guide (BWP001110)	$3.95	_____	_____
The Gospel of John: Light Overcoming Darkness, Part Two—Teaching Guide (BWP001111)	$4.50	_____	_____
The Book of Acts: Time to Act on Acts 1:8—Study Guide (BWP001142)	$3.95	_____	_____
The Book of Acts: Time to Act on Acts 1:8—Large Print Study Guide (BWP001143)	$4.25	_____	_____
The Book of Acts: Time to Act on Acts 1:8—Teaching Guide (BWP001144)	$4.95	_____	_____

Item	Price		
The Corinthian Letters—Study Guide (BWP001121)	$3.55	_____	_____
The Corinthian Letters—Large Print Study Guide (BWP001122)	$4.25	_____	_____
The Corinthian Letters—Teaching Guide (BWP001123)	$4.95	_____	_____
Galatians and 1&2 Thessalonians—Study Guide (BWP001080)	$3.55	_____	_____
Galatians and 1&2 Thessalonians—Large Print Study Guide (BWP001081)	$3.95	_____	_____
Galatians and 1&2 Thessalonians—Teaching Guide (BWP001082)	$3.95	_____	_____
Hebrews and the Letters of Peter—Study Guide (BWP001162)	$3.95	_____	_____
Hebrews and the Letters of Peter—Large Print Study Guide (BWP001163)	$4.25	_____	_____
Hebrews and the Letters of Peter—Teaching Guide (BWP001164)	$4.95	_____	_____
Letters of James and John—Study Guide (BWP001101)	$3.55	_____	_____
Letters of James and John—Large Print Study Guide (BWP001102)	$3.95	_____	_____
Letters of James and John—Teaching Guide (BWP001103)	$4.25	_____	_____

Coming for use beginning June 2014

Item	Price		
14 Habits of Highly Effective Disciples—Study Guide (BWP001177)	$3.95	_____	_____
14 Habits of Highly Effective Disciples—Large Print Study Guide (BWP001178)	$4.25	_____	_____
14 Habits of Highly Effective Disciples—Teaching Guide (BWP001179)	$4.95	_____	_____

Standard (UPS/Mail) Shipping Charges*			
Order Value	Shipping charge**	Order Value	Shipping charge**
$.01—$9.99	$6.50	$160.00—$199.99	$24.00
$10.00—$19.99	$8.50	$200.00—$249.99	$28.00
$20.00—$39.99	$9.50	$250.00—$299.99	$30.00
$40.00—$59.99	$10.50	$300.00—$349.99	$34.00
$60.00—$79.99	$11.50	$350.00—$399.99	$42.00
$80.00—$99.99	$12.50	$400.00—$499.99	$50.00
$100.00—$129.99	$15.00	$500.00—$599.99	$60.00
$130.00—$159.99	$20.00	$600.00—$799.99	$72.00**

Cost
of items (Order value) _____

Shipping charges
(see chart*) _____

TOTAL _____

*Please call 1-866-249-1799 if the exact amount is needed prior to ordering.

**For order values $800.00 and above, please call 1-866-249-1799 or check www.baptistwaypress.org

Please allow three weeks for standard delivery. For express shipping service: Call 1-866-249-1799 for information on additional charges.

YOUR NAME _____

PHONE _____

YOUR CHURCH _____

DATE ORDERED _____

SHIPPING ADDRESS _____

CITY _____

STATE _____ ZIP CODE _____

E-MAIL _____

MAIL this form with your check for the total amount to
BAPTISTWAY PRESS, Baptist General Convention of Texas,
333 North Washington, Dallas, TX 75246-1798
(Make checks to "BaptistWay Press")

OR, **CALL** your order toll-free: 1-866-249-1799
(M-Fri 8:30 a.m.-5:00 p.m. central time).

OR, **E-MAIL** your order to our internet e-mail address:
baptistway@texasbaptists.org.

OR, **ORDER ONLINE** at www.baptistwaypress.org.

We look forward to receiving your order! Thank you!